Richard, a Clown
Hostess of The Bell at Henley
Joan, a Country Wench
Constable
A Post
Spirit in the shape of Hercules
A Devil
Lords, Clowns, etc.

THE HONOURABLE HISTORY OF FRIAR BACON AND FRIAR BUNGAY

SCENE I

Near Framlingham.

Enter **PRINCE EDWARD**, malcontented, with **LACY**, **WARREN**, **ERMSBY** and **RALPH SIMNELL**.

LACY
Why looks my lord like to a troubled sky
When Heaven's bright shine is shadowed with a fog?
Alate we ran the deer, and through the lawnds
Stripped with our nags the lofty frolic bucks
That scudded 'fore the teasers like the wind:
Ne'er was the deer of merry Fressingfield
So lustily pulled down by jolly mates,
Nor shared the farmers such fat venison,
So frankly dealt, this hundred years before;
Nor have
I seen my lord more frolic in the chase,
And now changed to a melancholy dump.

WARREN
After the prince got to the Keeper's lodge,
And had been jocund in the house awhile,
Tossing off ale and milk in country cans,
Whether it was the country's sweet content,
Or else the bonny damsel filled us drink
That seemed so stately in her stammel red,
Or that a qualm did cross his stomach then,
But straight he fell into his passiöns.

ERMSBY
Sirrah Ralph, what say you to your master,
Shall he thus all amort live malcontent?

RALPH

Hearest thou, Ned?—Nay, look if he will speak to me!

PRINCE EDWARD
What say'st thou to me, fool?

RALPH
I prithee, tell me, Ned, art thou in love with the Keeper's daughter?

PRINCE EDWARD
How if I be, what then?

RALPH
Why, then, sirrah, I'll teach thee how to deceive Love.

PRINCE EDWARD
How, Ralph?

RALPH
Marry, Sirrah Ned, thou shall put on my cap and my coat and my dagger, and I will put on thy clothes and thy sword; and so thou shalt be my fool.

PRINCE EDWARD
And what of this?

RALPH
Why, so thou shalt beguile Love; for Love is such a proud scab, that he will never meddle with fools nor children. Is not Ralph's counsel good, Ned?

PRINCE EDWARD
Tell me, Ned Lacy, didst thou mark the maid,
How lovely in her country weeds she looked?
A bonnier wench all Suffolk cannot yield:—
All Suffolk! nay, all England holds none such.

RALPH
Sirrah Will Ermsby, Ned is deceived.

ERMSBY
Why, Ralph?

RALPH
He says all England hath no such, and I say, and I'll stand to it, there is one better in Warwickshire.

WARREN
How provest thou that, Ralph?

RALPH

The Honourable History of Friar Bacon & Friar Bungay by Robert Greene

As it was plaid by her Maiesties seruants.

Robert Greene was, by the best accounts available, born in Norwich in 1558 and baptised on July 11th.

Greene is believed to have been a pupil at Norwich Grammar School and then attended Cambridge receiving his B.A. in 1580, and an M.A. in 1583. He then moved to London and began an extraordinary chapter in his life as a widely published author.

His literary career began with the publication of the long romance, 'Mamillia', (1580). Greene's romances were written in a highly wrought style which reached its peak in 'Pandosto' (1588) and 'Menaphon' (1589). Short poems and songs incorporated in some of the romances attest to his ability as a lyric poet.

In 1588, he was granted an MA from Oxford University, almost certainly as a courtesy degree. Thereafter he sometimes placed the phrase Utruisq. Academiae in Artibus Magister', "Master of Arts in both Universities" on the title page of his works.

The lack of records hinders any complete biography of Greene but he did write an autobiography of sorts, but where the balance lies between facts and artistic licence is not clearly drawn. According to that autobiography 'The Repentance of Robert Greene', Greene is alleged to have written 'A Groatsworth of Wit Bought with a Million of Repentance' during the month prior to his death, including in it a letter to his wife asking her to forgive him and stating that he was sending their son back to her.

His output was prolific. Between 1583 and 1592, he published more than twenty-five works in prose, becoming one of the first authors in England to support himself with his pen in an era when professional authorship was virtually unknown.

In his 'coney-catching' pamphlets, Greene fashioned himself into a well-known public figure, narrating colourful inside stories of rakes and rascals duping young gentlemen and solid citizens out of their hard-earned money. These stories, told from the perspective of a repentant former rascal, have been considered autobiographical, and to incorporate many facts of Greene's own life thinly veiled as fiction. However, the alternate account suggests that Greene invented almost everything, merely displaying his undoubted skills as a writer.

In addition to his prose works, Greene also wrote several plays, none of them published in his lifetime, including 'The Scottish History of James IV', 'Alphonsus', and his greatest popular success, 'Friar Bacon and Friar Bungay', as well as 'Orlando Furioso', based on Ludovico Ariosto's Orlando Furioso.

His plays earned himself the title as one of the 'University Wits', a group that included George Peele, Thomas Nashe, and Christopher Marlowe.

Robert Greene died 3rd September 1592.

Index of Contents

DRAMATIS PERSONAE
King Henry the Third
Edward, Prince of Wales, his Son
Ralph Simnell, The King's Fool
Lacy, Earl of Lincoln
Warren, Earl of Sussex
Ermsby, a Gentleman
Friar Bacon
Miles, Friar Bacon's Poor Scholar
Friar Bungay
Emperor of Germany
King of Castile
Princess Elinor, Daughter to the King of Castile
Jaques Vandermast, A German Magician
Doctors of Oxford:
Burden
Mason
Clement
Lambert, a Gentleman
1st Scholar, Lambert's Son
Serlsby, a Gentleman
2nd Scholar, Serlsby's Son
Keeper
Margaret, the Keeper's Daughter
Thomas, a Clown

Why, is not the abbot a learned man, and hath read many books, and thinkest thou he hath not more learning than thou to choose a bonny wench?
Yes, warrant I thee, by his whole grammar.

ERMSBY
A good reason, Ralph.

PRINCE EDWARD
I tell thee, Lacy, that her sparkling eyes
Do lighten forth sweet love's alluring fire;
And in her tresses she doth fold the looks
Of such as gaze upon her golden hair:
Her bashful white, mixed with the morning's red,
Luna doth boast upon her lovely cheeks;
Her front is beauty's table, where she paints
The glories of her gorgeous excellence.
Her teeth are shelves of precious margarites,
Richly enclosed with ruddy coral cleeves.
Tush, Lacy, she is beauty's over-match,
If thou survey'st her curious imagery.

LACY
I grant, my lord, the damsel is as fair
As simple Suffolk's homely towns can yield.
But in the court be quainter dames than she,
Whose faces are enriched with honour's taint,
Whose beauties stand upon the stage of fame,
And vaunt their trophies in the courts of love.

PRINCE EDWARD
Ah, Ned, but hadst thou watch'd her as myself,
And seen the secret beauties of the maid,
Their courtly coyness were but foolery.

ERMSBY
Why, how watched you her, my lord?

PRINCE EDWARD
Whenas she swept like Venus through the house,
And in her shape fast folded up my thoughts,
Into the milk-house went I with the maid,
And there amongst the cream-bowls she did shine
As Pallas 'mongst her princely huswifery:
She turned her smock over her lily arms,
And dived them into milk to run her cheese;
But whiter than the milk her crystal skin,
Checkèd with lines of azure, made her blush
That art or nature durst bring for compare.

Ermsby,
If thou hadst seen, as I did note it well,
How beauty played the huswife, how this girl,
Like Lucrece, laid her fingers to the work,
Thou wouldst, with Tarquin, hazard Rome and all
To win the lovely maid of Fressingfield.

RALPH
Sirrah, Ned, wouldst fain have her?

PRINCE EDWARD
Ay, Ralph.

RALPH
Why, Ned, I have laid the plot in my head; thou shalt have her already.

PRINCE EDWARD
I'll give thee a new coat, an learn me that.

RALPH
Why, Sirrah Ned, we'll ride to Oxford to Friar Bacon: O, he is a brave scholar, sirrah; they say he is a brave necromancer, that he can make women of devils, and he can juggle cats into costermongers.

PRINCE EDWARD
And how then, Ralph?

RALPH
Marry, sirrah, thou shalt go to him: and because thy father Harry shall not miss thee, he shall turn me into thee; and I'll to the court, and I'll prince it out; and he shall make thee either a silken purse full of gold, or else a fine wrought smock.

PRINCE EDWARD
But how shall I have the maid?

RALPH
Marry, sirrah, if thou be'st a silken purse full of gold, then on Sundays she'll hang thee by her side, and you must not say a word. Now, sir, when she comes into a great prease of people, for fear of the cutpurse, on a sudden she'll swap thee into her plackerd; then, sirrah, being there, you may plead for yourself.

ERMSBY
Excellent policy!

PRINCE EDWARD
But how if I be a wrought smock?

RALPH

Then she'll put thee into her chest and lay thee into lavender, and upon some good day she'll put thee on; and at night when you go to bed, then being turned from a smock to a man, you may make up the match.

LACY
Wonderfully wisely counselled, Ralph.

PRINCE EDWARD
Ralph shall have a new coat.

RALPH
God thank you when I have it on my back,
Ned.

PRINCE EDWARD
Lacy, the fool hath laid a perfect plot,
For why our country Margaret is so coy,
And stands so much upon her honest points,
That marriage or no market with the maid—
Ermsby, it must be necromantic spells
And charms of art that must enchain her love,
Or else shall Edward never win the girl.
Therefore, my wags, we'll horse us in the morn,
And post to Oxford to this jolly friar:
Bacon shall by his magic do this deed.

WARREN
Content, my lord; and that's a speedy way
To wean these headstrong puppies from the teat.

PRINCE EDWARD
I am unknown, not taken for the prince;
They only deem us frolic courtiers,
That revel thus among our liege's game:
Therefore I have devised a policy.
Lacy, thou know'st next Friday is Saint James',
And then the country flocks to Harleston fair;
Then will the Keeper's daughter frolic there,
And over-shine the troop of all the maids
That come to see and to be seen that day.
Haunt thee disguised among the country-swains,
Feign thou'rt a farmer's son, not far from thence,
Espy her loves, and who she liketh best;
Cote him, and court her to control the clown;
Say that the courtier 'tirèd all in green,
That helped her handsomely to run her cheese,
And filled her father's lodge with venison,
Commends him, and sends fairings to herself.

Buy something worthy of her parentage,
Not worth her beauty; for, Lacy, then the fair
Affords no jewèl fitting for the maid.
And when thou talk's of me, note if she blush:
O, then she loves; but if her cheeks wax pale,
Disdain it is. Lacy, send how she fares,
And spare no time nor cost to win her loves.

LACY
I will, my lord, so execute this charge
As if that Lacy were in love with her.

PRINCE EDWARD
Send letters speedily to Oxford of the news.

RALPH
And, Sirrah Lacy, buy me a thousand thousand million of fine bells.

LACY
What wilt thou do with them, Ralph?

RALPH
Marry, every time that Ned sighs for the Keeper's daughter, I'll tie a bell about him: and so within three or four days I will send word to his father Harry, that his son, and my master Ned, is become Love's morris-dancer.

PRINCE EDWARD
Well, Lacy, look with care unto thy charge,
And I will haste to Oxford to the friar,
That he by art and thou by secret gifts
Mayst make me lord of merry Fressingfield.

LACY
God send your honour your heart's desire.

[Exeunt.

SCENE II

Friar Bacon's cell at Brasenose.

Enter **FRIAR BACON**, and **MILES**, his poor scholar with books under his arm; **BURDEN, MASON** and **CLEMENT**.

FRIAR BACON
Miles, where are you?

MILES

Hic sum, doctissime et reverendissime doctor.

FRIAR BACON

Attulisti nos libros meos de necromantia?

MILES

Ecce quam bonum et quam jucundum habitare libros in unum!

FRIAR BACON

Now, masters of our academic state
That rule in Oxford, viceroys in your place,
Whose heads contain maps of the liberal arts,
Spending your time in depth of learnèd skill,
Why flock you thus to Bacon's secret cell,
A friar newly stalled in Brazen-nose?
Say what's your mind, that I may make reply.

BURDEN

Bacon, we hear that long we have suspect,
That thou art read in magic's mystery;
In pyromancy, to divine by flames;
To tell, by hydromatic, ebbs and tides;
By aeromancy to discover doubts,
To plain out questions, as Apollo did.

FRIAR BACON

Well, Master Burden, what of all this?

MILES

Marry, sir, he doth but fulfil, by rehearsing of these names, the fable of the Fox and the Grapes; that which is above us pertains nothing to us.

BURDEN

I tell thee, Bacon, Oxford makes report,
Nay, England, and the court of Henry says,
Thou'rt making of a brazen head by art,
Which shall unfold strange doubts and aphorisms,
And read a lecture in philosophy;
And, by the help of devils and ghastly fiends,
Thou mean'st, ere many years or days be past,
To compass England with a wall of brass.

FRIAR BACON

And what of this?

MILES

What of this, master! Why, he doth speak mystically; for he knows, if your skill fail to make a brazen head, yet Mother Waters' strong ale will fit his turn to make him have a copper nose.

CLEMENT
Bacon, we come not grieving at thy skill,
But joying that our ácadémy yields
A man supposed the wonder of the world.
For if thy cunning work these miracles,
England and Europe shall admire thy fame,
And Oxford shall in characters of brass,
And statues, such as were built up in Rome,
Etérnize Friar Bacon for his art.

MASON
Then, gentle friar, tell us thy intent.

FRIAR BACON
Seeing you come as friends unto the friar,
Resolve you, doctors, Bacon can by books
Make storming Boreas thunder from his cave,
And dim fair Luna to a dark eclipse.
The great arch-ruler, potentate of hell,
Trembles when Bacon bids him, or his fiends,
Bow to the force of his pentageron.
What art can work, the frolic friar knows;
And therefore will I turn my magic books,
And strain out necromancy to the deep.
I have contrived and framed a head of brass
(I made Belcephon hammer out the stuff),
And that by art shall read philosophy.
And I will strengthen England by my skill,
That if ten Caesars lived and reigned in Rome,
With all the legions Europe doth contain,
They should not touch a grass of English ground;
The work that Ninus reared at Babylon,
The brazen walls framed by Semiramis,
Carved out like to the portal of the sun,
Shall not be such as rings the English strand
From Dover to the market-place of Rye.

BURDEN
Is this possible?

MILES
I'll bring ye two or three witnesses.

BURDEN
What be those?

MILES
Marry, sir, three or four as honest devils and good companions as any be in hell.

MASON
No doubt but magic may do much in this;
For he that reads but mathematic rules
Shall find conclusions that avail to work
Wonders that pass the common sense of men.

BURDEN
But Bacon roves a bow beyond his reach,
And tells of more than magic can perform,
Thinking to get a fame by fooleries.
Have I not passed as far in state of schools,
And read of many secrets ? Yet to think
That heads of brass can utter any voice,
Or more, to tell of deep philosophy,
This is a fable Æsop had forgot.

FRIAR BACON
Burden, thou wrong'st me in detracting thus;
Bacon loves not to stuff himself with lies.
But tell me 'fore these doctors, if thou dare,
Of certain questions I shall move to thee.

BURDEN
I will: ask what thou can.

MILES
Marry, sir, he'll straight be on your pick-pack to know whether the feminine or the masculine gender be most worthy.

FRIAR BACON
Were you not yesterday, Master Burden, at
Henley upon the Thames?

BURDEN
I was: what then?

FRIAR BACON
What book studied you thereon all night?

BURDEN
I! None at all; I read not there a line.

FRIAR BACON
Then, doctors, Friar Bacon's art knows naught.

CLEMENT
What say you to this, Master Burden? Doth he not touch you?

BURDEN
I pass not of his frivolous speeches.

MILES
Nay, Master Burden, my master, ere he hath done with you, will turn you from a doctor to a dunce, and shake you so small that he will leave no more learning in you than is in Balaam's ass.

FRIAR BACON
Masters, for that learnèd Burden's skill is deep,
And sore he doubts of Bacon's cabalism,
I'll show you why he haunts to Henley oft.
Not, doctors, for to taste the fragrant air,
But there to spend the night in alchemy,
To multiply with secret spells of art;
Thus private steals he learning from us all.
To prove my sayings true, I'll show you straight
The book he keeps at Henley for himself.

MILES
Nay, now my master goes to conjuration, take heed.

FRIAR BACON
Masters,
Stand still, fear not, I'll show you but his book.

[Conjures.

Per omnes deos infernales, Belcephon!

[Enter **HOSTESS** with a shoulder of mutton on a spit, and a **DEVIL**.

MILES
Oh, master, cease your conjuration, or you spoil all; for here's a she-devil come with a shoulder of mutton on a spit. You have marred the devil's supper; but no doubt he thinks our college fare is slender, and so hath sent you his cook with a shoulder of mutton, to make it exceed.

HOSTESS
O, where am I, or what's become of me?

FRIAR BACON
What art thou?

HOSTESS
Hostess at Henley, mistress of the Bell.

FRIAR BACON
How cam'st thou here?

WOMAN
As I was in the kitchen 'mongst the maids,
Spitting the meat 'gainst supper for my guess,
A motion moved me to look forth of door:
No sooner had I pried into the yard,
But straight a whirlwind hoisted me from thence,
And mounted me aloft unto the clouds.
As in a trance I thought nor fearèd naught,
Nor know I where or whither I was ta'en,
Nor where I am nor what these persons be.

FRIAR BACON
No? Know you not Master Burden?

WOMAN
O, yes, good sir, he is my daily guest.—
What, Master Burden! 'twas but yesternight
That you and I at Henley played at cards.

BURDEN
I know not what we did.—A pox of all conjuring friars!

CLEMENT
Now, jolly friar, tell us, is this the book
That Burden is so careful to look on?

FRIAR BACON
It is.—But, Burden, tell me now,
Think'st thou that Bacon's necromantic skill
Cannot perform his head and wall of brass,
When he can fetch thine hostess in such post!

MILES
I'll warrant you, master, if Master Burden could conjure as well as you, he would have his book every night from Henley to study on at Oxford.

MASON
Burden,
What, are you mated by this frolic friar?—
Look how he droops; his guilty consciënce
Drives him to bash, and makes his hostess blush.

FRIAR BACON
Well, mistress, for I will not have you missed,

You shall to Henley to cheer up your guests
Fore supper gin.—Burden, bid her adieu;
Say farewell to your hostess 'fore she goes.—
Sirrah, away, and set her safe at home.

HOSTESS
Master Burden, when shall we see you at
Henley?

BURDEN
The devil take thee and Henley too.

[Exeunt **HOSTESS** and **DEVIL**.

MILES
Master, shall I make a good motion?

FRIAR BACON
What's that?

MILES
Marry, sir, now that my hostess is gone to provide supper, conjure up another spirit, and send Doctor
Burden flying after.

FRIAR BACON
Thus, rulers of our academic state,
You have seen the friar frame his art by proof;
And as the college callèd Brazen-nose
Is under him, and he the master there,
So surely shall this head of brass be framed,
And yield forth strange and uncouth aphorisms;
And hell and Hecatë shall fail the friar,
But I will circle England round with brass.

MILES
So be it et nunc et semper; amen.

[Exeunt.

SCENE III

The Harleston Fair.

Enter **MARGARET** and **JOAN**; **THOMAS**, **RICHARD** and other **CLOWNS**; and **LACY** disguised in country
apparel.

THOMAS

By my troth, Margaret, here's a weather is able to make a man call his father "whoreson": if this weather hold, we shall have hay good cheap, and butter and cheese at Harleston will bear no price.

MARGARET

Thomas, maids when they come to see the fair
Count not to make a cope for dearth of hay:
When we have turned our butter to the salt,
And set our cheese safely upon the racks,
Then let our fathers prize it as they please.
We country sluts of merry Fressingfield
Come to buy needless naughts to make us fine,
And look that young men should be frank this day,
And court us with such fairings as they can.
Phoebus is blithe, and frolic looks from Heaven,
As when he courted lovely Semele,
Swearing the pedlars shall have empty packs,
If that fair weather may make chapmen buy.

LACY

But, lovely Peggy, Semele is dead,
And therefore Phoebus from his palace pries,
And, seeing such a sweet and seemly saint,
Shows all his glories for to court yourself.

MARGARET

This is a fairing, gentle sir, indeed,
To soothe me up with such smooth flattery;
But learn of me, your scoff's too broad before.—
Well, Joan, our beauties must abide their jests;
We serve the turn in jolly Fressingfield.

JOAN

Margaret,
A farmer's daughter for a farmer's son:
I warrant you, the meanest of us both
Shall have a mate to lead us from the church.

[**LUCY** whispers **MARGARET** in the ear.

But, Thomas, what's the news? What, in a dump?
Give me your hand, we are near a pedlar's shop;
Out with your purse, we must have fairings now.

THOMAS

Faith, Joan, and shall. I'll bestow a fairing on you, and then we will to the tavern, and snap off a pint of wine or two.

MARGARET
Whence are you, sir! Of Suffolk? For your terms
Are finer than the common sort of men.

LACY
Faith, lovely girl, I am of Beccles by,
Your neighbour, not above six miles from hence,
A farmer's son, that never was so quaint
But that he could do courtesy to such dames.
But trust me, Margaret, I am sent in charge
From him that revelled in your father's house,
And filled his lodge with cheer and venison,
'Tirèd in green: he sent you this rich purse,
His token that he helped you run your cheese,
And in the milkhouse chatted with yourself.

MARGARET
To me?

LACY
You forget yourself:
Women are often weak in memory.

MARGARET
O, pardon, sir, I call to mind the man:
'Twere little manners to refuse his gift,
And yet I hope he sends it not for love;
For we have little leisure to debate of that.

JOAN
What, Margaret! blush not; maids must have their loves.

THOMAS
Nay, by the mass, she looks pale as if she were angry.

RICHARD
Sirrah, are you of Beccles? I pray, how doth
Goodman Cob? My father bought a horse of him.—
I'll tell you, Margaret, 'a were good to be a gentleman's jade, for of all things the foul hilding could not
abide a dung-cart.

MARGARET [Aside]
How different is this farmer from the rest
That erst as yet hath pleased my wandering sight!
His words are witty, quickened with a smile,
His courtesy gentle, smelling of the court;
Facile and debonair in all his deeds;
Proportioned as was Paris, when, in grey,

He courted Œnon in the vale by Troy.
Great lords have come and pleaded for my love:
Who but the Keeper's lass of Fressingfield?
And yet methinks this farmer's jolly son
Passeth the proudest that hath pleased mine eye.
But, Peg, disclose not that thou art in love,
And show as yet no sign of love to him,
Although thou well wouldst wish him for thy love:
Keep that to thee till time doth serve thy turn,
To show the grief wherein thy heart doth burn.—
Come, Joan and Thomas, shall we to the fair?—
You, Beccles man, will not forsake us now?

LACY
Not whilst I may have such quaint girls as you.

MARGARET
Well, if you chance to come by Fressingfield,
Make but a step into the Keeper's lodge,
And such poor fare as woodmen can afford,
Butter and cheese, cream and fat venison,
You shall have store, and welcome therewithal.

LACY
Gramercies, Peggy; look for me ere long.

[Exeunt.

SCENE IV

The Court at Hampton-House.

Enter **KING HENRY THE THIRD**, the **EMPEROR**, the **KING OF CASTILE**, **ELINOR**, and **VANDERMAST**.

KING HENRY
Great men of Europe, monarchs of the west,
Ringed with the walls of old Oceänus,
Whose lofty surges like the battlements
That compassed high-built Babel in with towers,
Welcome, my lords, welcome, brave western kings,
To England's shore, whose promontory-cleeves
Show Albion is another little world;
Welcome says English Henry to you all;
Chiefly unto the lovely Elinor,
Who dared for Edward's sake cut through the seas,
And venture as Agenor's damsel through the deep,

To get the love of Henry's wanton son.

KING OF CASTILE
England's rich monarch, brave Plantagenet,
The Pyren Mounts, swelling above the clouds,
That ward the wealthy Castile in with walls,
Could not detain the beauteous Elinor;
But hearing of the fame of Edward's youth,
She dared to brook Neptunus' haughty pride,
And bide the brunt of froward Æolus:
Then may fair England welcome her the more.

ELINOR
After that English Henry by his lords
Had sent Prince Edward's lovely counterfeit,
A present to the Castile Elinor,
The comely portrait of so brave a man,
The virtuous fame discoursèd of his deeds,
Edward's courageous resolutiön,
Done at the Holy Land 'fore Damas' walls,
Led both mine eye and thoughts in equal links,
To like so of the English monarch's son,
That I attempted perils for his ease.

EMPEROR
Where is the prince, my lord?

KING HENRY
He posted down, not long since, from the court,
To Suffolk side, to merry Fremingham,
To sport himself amongst my fallow deer:
From thence, by packets sent to Hampton house,
We hear the prince is ridden, with his lords,
To Oxford, in the ácadémy there
To hear dispute amongst the learnèd men.
But we will send forth letters for my son,
To will him come from Oxford to the court.

EMPEROR
Nay, rather, Henry, let us, as we be,
Ride for to visit Oxford with our train.
Fain would I see your universities,
And what learn'd men your ácadémy yields.
From Hapsburg have I brought a learnèd clerk
To hold dispute with English orators—
This doctor, surnamed Jaques Vandermast,
A German born, passed into Padua,
To Florence and to fair Bolognia,

To Paris, Rheims, and stately Orleans,
And, talking there with men of art, put down
The chiefest of them all in aphorisms,
In magic, and the mathematic rules:
Now let us, Henry, try him in your schools.

KING HENRY
He shall, my lord; this motion likes me well.
We'll progress straight to Oxford with our trains,
And see what men our ácadémy brings.—
And, wonder Vandermast, welcome to me;
In Oxford shall thou find a jolly friar,
Called Friar Bacon, England's only flower:
Set him but nonplus in his magic spells,
And make him yield in mathematic rules,
And for thy glory I will bind thy brows,
Not with a poet's garland made of bays,
But with a coronet of choicest gold.
Whilst then we fit to Oxford with our troops,
Let's in and banquet in our English court.

[Exeunt.

SCENE V

Oxford.

Enter **RALPH SIMNELL** in Prince Edward's apparel; and **PRINCE EDWARD**, **WARREN**, and **ERMSBY**, disguised.

RALPH
Where be these vagabond knaves, that they attend no better on their master?

PRINCE EDWARD
If it please your honour, we are all ready at an inch.

RALPH
Sirrah Ned, I'll have no more post-horse to ride on: I'll have another fetch.

ERMSBY
I pray you, how is that, my lord?

RALPH
Marry, sir, I'll send to the Isle of Ely for four or five dozen of geese, and I'll have them tied six and six together with whip cord: now upon their backs will I have a fair field-bed with a canopy; and so, when it is my pleasure, I'll flee into what place I please. This will be easy.

WARREN
Your honour hath said well; but shall we to
Brazen-nose College before we pull off our boots?

ERMSBY
Warren, well motioned; we will to the friar
Before we revel it within the town.—
Ralph, see you keep your countenance like a prince.

RALPH
Wherefore have I such a company of cutting knaves to wait upon me, but to keep and defend my
countenance against all mine enemies; have you not good swords and bucklers?

ERMSBY
Stay, who comes here?

WARREN
Some scholar; and we'll ask him where
Friar Bacon is.

[Enter **FRIAR BACON** and **MILES**.

FRIAR BACON
Why, thou arrant dunce, shall I never make thee a good scholar? doth not all the town cry out and say,
Friar Bacon's subsizer is the greatest blockhead in all Oxford? Why, thou canst not speak one word of
true Latin.

MILES
No, sir? Yet, what is this else? Ego sum tuus homo, "I am your man": I warrant you, sir, as good Tully's
phrase as any is in Oxford.

FRIAR BACON
Come on, sirrah; what part of speech is Ego?

MILES
Ego, that is "I"; marry, nomen substantivo.

FRIAR BACON
How prove you that?

MILES
Why, sir, let him prove himself an 'a will; I can be heard, felt, and understood.

FRIAR BACON
O gross dunce!

[Beats him.

PRINCE EDWARD
Come, let us break off this dispute between these two.—Sirrah, where is Brazen-nose College?

MILES
Not far from Coppersmith's Hall.

PRINCE EDWARD
What, dost thou mock me?

MILES
Not I, sir: but what would you at Brazen-nose?

ERMSBY
Marry, we would speak with Friar Bacon.

MILES
Whose men be you?

ERMSBY
Marry, scholar, here's our master.

RALPH
Sirrah, I am the master of these good fellows; mayst thou not know me to be a lord by my reparrel?

MILES
Then here's good game for the hawk; for here's the master-fool and a covey of coxcombs: one wise man, I think, would spring you all.

PRINCE EDWARD
Gog's wounds! Warren, kill him.

WARREN
Why, Ned, I think the devil be in my sheath;
I cannot get out my dagger.

ERMSBY
Nor I mine! 'Swones, Ned, I think I am bewitched.

MILES
A company of scabs! The proudest of you all draw your weapon, if he can.—
[Aside]
See how boldly I speak, now my master is by.

PRINCE EDWARD
I strive in vain; but if my sword be shut
And conjured fast by magic in my sheath,
Villain, here is my fist.

[Strikes **MILES** a box on the ear.

MILES
Oh, I beseech you conjure his hands too, that he may not lift his arms to his head, for he is light-fingered!

RALPH
Ned, strike him; I'll warrant thee by mine honour.

FRIAR BACON
What means the English prince to wrong my man?

PRINCE EDWARD
To whom speak'st thou?

FRIAR BACON
To thee.

PRINCE EDWARD
Who art thou?

FRIAR BACON
Could you not judge when all your swords grew fast,
That Friar Bacon was not far from hence?
Edward, King Henry's son and Prince of Wales,
Thy fool disguised cannot conceal thyself.
I know both Ermsby and the Sussex Earl,
Else Friar Bacon had but little skill.
Thou com'st in post from merry Fressingfield,
Fast-fancied to the Keeper's bonny lass,
To crave some succour of the jolly friar:—
And Lacy, Earl of Lincoln, hast thou left
To treat fair Margaret to allow thy loves;
But friends are men, and love can baffle lords;
The earl both woos and courts her for himself.

WARREN
Ned, this is strange; the friar knoweth all.

ERMSBY
Apollo could not utter more than this.

PRINCE EDWARD
I stand amazed to hear this jolly friar
Tell even the very secrets of my thoughts.—
But, learnèd Bacon, since thou know'st the cause
Why I did post so fast from Fressingfield,

Help, friar, at a pinch, that I may have
The love of lovely Margaret to myself,
And, as I am true Prince of Wales, I'll give
Living and lands to strength thy college-state.

WARREN
Good friar, help the prince in this.

RALPH
Why, servant Ned, will not the friar do it? Were not my sword glued to my scabbard by conjuration, I would cut off his head, and make him do it by force.

MILES
In faith, my lord, your manhood and your sword is all alike; they are so fast conjured that we shall never see them.

ERMSBY
What, doctor, in a dump! tush, help the prince,
And thou shalt see how liberal he will prove.

FRIAR BACON
Crave not such actions greater dumps than these?
I will, my lord, strain out my magic spells;
For this day comes the earl to Fressingfield,
And 'fore that night shuts in the day with dark,
They'll be betrothèd each to other fast.
But come with me; we'll to my study straight,
And in a glass prospective I will show
What's done this day in merry Fressingfield.

PRINCE EDWARD
Gramercies, Bacon; I will quite thy pain.

FRIAR BACON
But send your train, my lord, into the town:
My scholar shall go bring them to their inn;
Meanwhile we'll see the knavery of the earl.

PRINCE EDWARD
Warren, leave me;—and, Ermsby, take the fool:
Let him be master, and go revel it,
Till I and Friar Bacon talk awhile.

WARREN
We will, my lord.

RALPH
Faith, Ned, and I'll lord it out till thou comest:

I'll be Prince of Wales over all the black-pots in
Oxford.

[Exeunt **WARREN**, **ERMSBY**, **RALPH SIMNELL** and **MILES**.

[**FRIAR BACON** and **PRINCE EDWARD** go into the study.

SCENE VI

Friar Bacon's Study.

FRIAR BACON
Now, frolic Edward, welcome to my cell;
Here tempers Friar Bacon many toys,
And holds this place his cónsistory-court,
Wherein the devils plead homage to his words.
Within this glass prospective thou shalt see
This day what's done in merry Fressingfield
'Twixt lovely Peggy and the Lincoln Earl.

PRINCE EDWARD
Friar, thou glad'st me: now shall Edward try
How Lacy meaneth to his sovereign Lord.

FRIAR BACON
Stand there and look directly in the glass.

[Enter **MARGARET** and **FRIAR BUNGAY**.

What sees my lord?

PRINCE EDWARD
I see the Keeper's lovely lass appear,
As brightsome as the paramour of Mars,
Only attended by a jolly friar.

FRIAR BACON
Sit still, and keep the crystal in your eye.

MARGARET
But tell me, Friar Bungay, is it true
That this fair courteous country swain,
Who says his father is a farmer nigh,
Can be Lord Lacy, Earl of Lincolnshire?

FRIAR BUNGAY

Peggy, 'tis true, 'tis Lacy for my life,
Or else mine art and cunning both do fail,
Left by Prince Edward to procure his loves;
For he in green, that holp you run your cheese,
Is son to Henry and the Prince of Wales.

MARGARET
Be what he will, his lure is but for lust.
But did Lord Lacy like poor Margaret,
Or would he deign to wed a country lass,
Friar, I would his humble handmaid be,
And for great wealth quite him with courtesy.

FRIAR BUNGAY
Why, Margaret, dost thou love him?

MARGARET
His personage, like the pride of vaunting Troy,
Might well avouch to shadow Helen's rape:
His wit is quick and ready in conceit,
As Greece afforded in her chiefest prime:
Courteous, ah friar, full of pleasing smiles!
Trust me, I love too much to tell thee more;
Suffice to me he's England's paramour.

FRIAR BUNGAY
Hath not each eye that viewed thy pleasing face
Surnamèd thee Fair Maid of Fressingfield?

MARGARET
Yes, Bungay; and would God the lovely earl
Had that in esse that so many sought.

FRIAR BUNGAY
Fear not, the friar will not be behind
To show his cunning to entangle love.

PRINCE EDWARD
I think the friar courts the bonny wench:
Bacon, methinks he is a lusty churl.

FRIAR BACON
Now look, my lord.

[Enter **LACY** disguised as before.

PRINCE EDWARD
Gog's wounds, Bacon, here comes Lacy!

FRIAR BACON

Sit still, my lord, and mark the comedy.

FRIAR BUNGAY

Here's Lacy, Margaret; step aside awhile.

[Retires with **MARGARET**.

LACY

Daphne, the damsel that caught Phoebus fast,
And locked him in the brightness of her looks,
Was not so beauteous in Apollo's eyes
As is fair Margaret to the Lincoln Earl.—
Recant thee, Lacy, thou art put in trust:
Edward, thy sovereign's son, hath chosen thee,
A secret friend, to court her for himself,
And dar'st thou wrong thy prince with treachery?
Lacy, love makes no exception of a friend,
Nor deems it of a prince but as a man.
Honour bids thee control him in his lust;
His wooing is not for to wed the girl,
But to entrap her and beguile the lass.
Lacy, thou lov'st, then brook not such abuse,
But wed her, and abide thy prince's frown;
For better die than see her live disgraced.

MARGARET

Come, friar, I will shake him from his dumps.—
How cheer you, sir? A penny for your thought:
You 're early up, pray God it be the near.
What, come from Beccles in the morn so soon?

LACY

Thus watchful are such men as live in love,
Whose eyes brook broken slumbers for their sleep.
I tell thee, Peggy, since last Harleston fair
My mind hath felt a heap of passiöns.

MARGARET

A trusty man, that court it for your friend;
Woo you still for the courtier all in green?
I marvel that he sues not for himself.

LACY

Peggy,
I pleaded first to get your grace for him;
But when mine eyes surveyed your beauteous looks,

Love, like a wag, straight dived into my heart,
And there did shrine th' idea of yourself.
Pity me, though I be a farmer's son,
And measure not my riches, but my love.

MARGARET
You are very hasty; for to garden well,
Seeds must have time to sprout before they spring:
Love ought to creep as doth the dial's shade,
For timely ripe is rotten too-too soon.

FRIAR BUNGAY [Coming forward]
Deus hic; room for a merry friar!
What, youth of Beccles, with the Keeper's lass?
'Tis well; but tell me, hear you any news?

MARGARET
No, friar: what news?

FRIAR BUNGAY
Hear you not how the pursuivants do post
With proclamations through each country-town?

LACY
For what, gentle friar? Tell the news.

FRIAR BUNGAY
Dwell'st thou in Beccles, and hear'st not of these news?
Lacy, the Earl of Lincoln, is late fled
From Windsor court, disguisèd like a swain,
And lurks about the country here unknown.
Henry suspects him of some treachery,
And therefore doth proclaim in every way
That who can take the Lincoln Earl shall have,
Paid in th' Exchequer, twenty thousand crowns.

LACY
The Earl of Lincoln! Friar, thou art mad:
It was some other; thou mistak'st the man.
The Earl of Lincoln! Why, it cannot be.

MARGARET
Yes, very well, my lord, for you are he:
The Keeper's daughter took you prisoner.
Lord Lacy, yield, I'll be your gaoler once.

PRINCE EDWARD
How familiar they be, Bacon!

FRIAR BACON
Sit still, and mark the sequel of their loves.

LACY
Then am I double prisoner to thyself:
Peggy, I yield. But are these news in jest?

MARGARET
In jest with you, but earnest unto me;
For why these wrongs do wring me at the heart.
Ah, how these earls and noblemen of birth
Flatter and feign to forge poor women's ill!

LACY
Believe me, lass, I am the Lincoln Earl:
I not deny but, 'tirèd thus in rags,
I lived disguised to win fair Peggy's love.

MARGARET
What love is there where wedding ends not love?

LACY
I mean, fair girl, to make thee Lacy's wife.

MARGARET
I little think that earls will stoop so low.

LACY
Say shall I make thee countess ere I sleep?

MARGARET
Handmaid unto the earl, so please himself:
A wife in name, but servant in obedience.

LACY
The Lincoln Countess, for it shall be so;
I'll plight the bands, and seal it with a kiss.

PRINCE EDWARD
Gog's wounds, Bacon, they kiss! I'll stab them.

FRIAR BACON
O, hold your hands, my lord, it is the glass!

PRINCE EDWARD
Choler to see the traitors gree so well
Made me to think the shadows substances.

FRIAR BACON

'Twere a long poniard, my lord, to reach between
Oxford and Fressingfield; but sit still and see more.

FRIAR BUNGAY

Well, Lord of Lincoln, if your loves be knit,
And that your tongues and thoughts do both agree,
To avoid ensuing jars, I'll hamper up the match.
I'll take my portace forth and wed you here;
Then go to bed and seal up your desires.

LACY

Friar, content.—Peggy, how like you this?

MARGARET

What likes my lord is pleasing unto me.

FRIAR BUNGAY

Then hand-fast hand, and I will to my book.

FRIAR BACON

What sees my lord now?

PRINCE EDWARD

Bacon, I see the lovers hand in hand,
The friar ready with his portace there
To wed them both: then am I quite undone.
Bacon, help now, if e'er thy magic served;
Help, Bacon; stop the marriage now,
If devils or necromancy may suffice,
And I will give thee forty thousand crowns.

FRIAR BACON

Fear not, my lord, I'll stop the jolly friar
For mumbling up his orisons this day.

[**FRIAR BUNGAY** is mute, crying "Hud, hud.

LACY

Why speak'st not, Bungay? Friar, to thy book.

MARGARET

How look'st thou, friar, as a man distraught?
Reft of thy senses, Bungay? Show by signs,
If thou be dumb, what passions holdeth thee.

LACY

He's dumb indeed. Bacon hath with his devils
Enchanted him, or else some strange disease
Or apoplexy hath possessed his lungs:
But, Peggy, what he cannot with his book,
We'll 'twixt us both unite it up in heart.

MARGARET
Else let me die, my lord, a miscreant.

PRINCE EDWARD
Why stands Friar Bungay so amazed?

FRIAR BACON
I have struck him dumb, my lord; and if your honour please,
I'll fetch this Bungay straightway from Fressingfield,
And he shall dine with us in Oxford here.

PRINCE EDWARD
Bacon, do that, and thou contentest me.

LACY
Of courtesy, Margaret, let us lead the friar
Unto thy father's lodge, to comfort him
With broths to bring him from this hapless trance.

MARGARET
Or else, my lord, we were passing unkind
To leave this friar so in his distress.

[Enter a **DEVIL**, who carries off **FRIAR BUNGAY** on his back.

O, help, my lord! A devil, a devil, my lord!
Look how he carries Bungay on his back!
Let's hence, for Bacon's spirits be abroad.

[Exit with **LACY**.

PRINCE EDWARD
Bacon, I laugh to see the jolly friar
Mounted upon the devil, and how the earl
Flees with his bonny lass for fear.
As soon as Bungay is at Brazen-nose,
And I have chatted with the merry friar,
I will in post hie me to Fressingfield,
And quite these wrongs on Lacy ere't be long.

FRIAR BACON
So be it my lord: but let us to our dinner;

For ere we have taken our repast awhile,
We shall have Bungay brought to Brazen-nose.

[Exeunt.

The Regent House at Oxford.

Enter **BURDEN**, **MASON** and **CLEMENT**.

MASON
Now that we are gathered in the Regent-house,
It fits us talk about the king's repair,
For he, troopèd with all the western kings,
That lie alongst the Dantzic seas by east,
North by the clime of frosty Germany,
The Almain monarch, and the Scocun duke,
Castile and lovely Elinor with him,
Have in their jests resolved for Oxford town.

BURDEN
We must lay plots of stately tragedies,
Strange comic shows, such as proud Roscius
Vaunted before the Roman emperors,
To welcome all the western potentates.

CLEMENT
But more; the king by letters hath foretold
That Frederick, the Almain emperor,
Hath brought with him a German of esteem,
Whose surname is Don Jaques Vandermast,
Skilful in magic and those secret arts.

MASON
Then must we all make suit unto the friar,
To Friar Bacon, that he vouch this task,
And undertake to countervail in skill
The German; else there's none in Oxford can
Match and dispute with learnèd Vandermast.

BURDEN
Bacon, if he will hold the German play,
Will teach him what an English friar can do:
The devil, I think, dare not dispute with him.

CLEMENT
Indeed, Mas Doctor, he [dis]pleasured you,
In that he brought your hostess with her spit,
From Henley, posting unto Brazen-nose.

BURDEN
A vengeance on the friar for his pains!
But leaving that, let's hie to Bacon straight,
To see if he will take this task in hand.

CLEMENT
Stay, what rumour is this? The town is up in
a mutiny: what hurly-burly is this?

[Enter a **CONSTABLE**, with **RALPH SIMNELL**, **WARREN**, **ERMSBY**, all three disguised as before, and **MILES**.

CONSTABLE
Nay, masters, if you were ne'er so good, you shall before the doctors to answer your misdemeanour.

BURDEN
What's the matter, fellow?

CONSTABLE
Marry, sir, here's a company of rufflers, that, drinking in the tavern, have made a great brawl and almost killed the vintner.

MILES
Salve, Doctor Burden!
This lubberly lurden
Ill-shaped and ill-faced,
Disdained and disgraced,
What he tells unto vobis,
Mentitur de nobis.

BURDEN
Who is the master and chief of this crew?

MILES
Ecce asinum mundi,
Figura rotundi,
Neat, sheat, and fine,
As brisk as a cup of wine.

BURDEN
What are you?

RALPH

I am, father doctor, as a man would say, the bell-wether of this company: these are my lords, and I the Prince of Wales.

CLEMENT
Are you Edward, the king's son?

RALPH
Sirrah Miles, bring hither the tapster that drew the wine, and, I warrant, when they see how soundly I have broke his head, they'll say 'twas done by no less man than a prince.

MASON
I cannot believe that this is the Prince of Wales.

WARREN
And why so, sir?

MASON
For they say the prince is a brave and a wise gentleman.

WARREN
Why, and think'st thou, doctor, that he is not so?
Dar'st thou detract and derogate from him,
Being so lovely and so brave a youth?

ERMSBY
Whose face, shining with many a sugared smile,
Bewrays that he is bred of princely race.

MILES
And yet, master doctor,
To speak like a proctor,
And tell unto you
What is veriment and true;
To cease of this quarrel,
Look but on his apparel;
Then mark but my talis,
He is great Prince of Walis,
The chief of our gregis,
And filius regis:
Then 'ware what is done,
For he is Henry's white son.

RALPH
Doctors, whose doting night-caps are not capable of my ingenious dignity, know that I am Edward Plantagenet, whom if you displease, will make a ship that shall hold all your colleges, and so carry away the niniversity with a fair wind to the Bankside in Southwark.—How sayest thou, Ned Warren, shall I not do it?

WARREN
Yes, my good lord; and, if it please your lordship, I will gather up all your old pantofles, and with the cork make you a pinnace of five-hundred ton, that shall serve the turn marvelous well, my lord.

ERMSBY
And I, my lord, will have pioners to undermine the town, that the very gardens and orchards be carried away for your summer-walks.

MILES
And I, with scientia,
And great diligentia,
Will conjure and charm,
To keep you from harm;
That utrum horum mavis,
Your very great navis,
Like Bartlett's ship,
From Oxford do skip
With colleges and schools,
Full-loaden with fools.
Quid dicis ad hoc,
Worshipful Domine Dawcock?

CLEMENT
Why, hare-brained courtiers, are you drunk or mad,
To taunt us up with such scurrility?
Deem you us men of base and light esteem,
To bring us such a fop for Henry's son?—
Call out the beadles and convey them hence
Straight to Bocardo: let the roisters lie
Close clapt in bolts, until their wits be tame.

ERMSBY
Why, shall we to prison, my lord?

RALPH
What sayest, Miles, shall I honour the prison with my presence?

MILES
No, no; out with your blades,
And hamper these jades;
Have a flurt and a crash,
Now play revel-dash,
And teach these sacerdos
That the Bocardos,
Like peasants and elves,
Are meet for themselves.

MASON

To the prison with them, constable.

WARREN
Well, doctors, seeing I have sported me
With laughing at these mad and merry-wags,
Know that Prince Edward is at Brazen-nose,
And this, attirèd like the Prince of Wales,
Is Ralph, King Henry's only lovèd fool;
I, Earl of Sussex, and this Ermsby,
One of the privy-chamber to the king;
Who, while the prince with Friar Bacon stays,
Have revelled it in Oxford as you see.

MASON
My lord, pardon us, we knew not what you were:
But courtiers may make greater scapes than these.
Wilt please your honour dine with me to-day?

WARREN
I will, Master Doctor, and satisfy the vintner for his hurt; only I must desire you to imagine him all this
forenoon the Prince of Wales.

MASON
I will, sir.

RALPH
And upon that I will lead the way; only I will have Miles go before me, because I have heard Henry say
that wisdom must go before majesty.

[Exeunt.

Fressingfield.

Enter **PRINCE EDWARD** with his poniard in his hand, **LACY**, and **MARGARET**.

PRINCE EDWARD
Lacy, thou canst not shroud thy traitorous thoughts,
Nor cover, as did Cassius, all thy wiles;
For Edward hath an eye that looks as far
As Lynceus from the shores of Græcia.
Did not I sit in Oxford by the friar,
And see thee court the maid of Fressingfield,
Sealing thy flattering fancies with a kiss?
Did not proud Bungay draw his portace forth,

And joining hand in hand had married you,
If Friar Bacon had not stroke him dumb,
And mounted him upon a spirit's back,
That we might chat at Oxford with the friar?
Traitor, what answer'st! Is not all this true?

LACY
Truth all, my lord; and thus I make reply.
At Harleston Fair, there courting for your grace,
Whenas mine eye surveyed her curious shape,
And drew the beauteous glory of her looks
To dive into the centre of my heart,
Love taught me that your honour did but jest,
That princes were in fancy but as men;
How that the lovely maid of Fressingfield
Was fitter to be Lacy's wedded wife
Than concubine unto the Prince of Wales.

PRINCE EDWARD
Injurious Lacy, did I love thee more
Than Alexander his Hephæstiön?
Did I unfold the passions of my love,
And lock them in the closet of thy thoughts?
Wert thou to Edward second to himself,
Sole friend, and partner of his secret loves?
And could a glance of fading beauty break
Th' enchainèd fetters of such private friends?
Base coward, false, and too effeminate
To be corrival with a prince in thoughts!
From Oxford have I posted since I dined,
To quite a traitor 'fore that Edward sleep.

MARGARET
'Twas I, my lord, not Lacy, stept awry.
For oft he sued and courted for yourself,
And still wooed for the courtier all in green;
But I, whom fancy made but over-fond,
Pleaded myself with looks as if I loved.
I fed mine eye with gazing on his face,
And still bewitched loved Lacy with my looks;
My heart with sighs, mine eyes pleaded with tears,
My face held pity and content at once,
And more I could not cipher-out by signs,
But that I loved Lord Lacy with my heart.
Then, worthy Edward, measure with thy mind
If women's favours will not force men fall;
If beauty, and if darts of piercing love,
Are not offered to bury thoughts of friends.

PRINCE EDWARD

I tell thee, Peggy, I will have thy loves;
Edward or none shall conquer Margaret.
In frigates bottomed with rich Sethin planks,
Topt with the lofty firs of Lebanon,
Stemmed and incased with burnished ivory,
And over-laid with plates of Persian wealth,
Like Thetis shall thou wanton on the waves,
And draw the dolphins to thy lovely eyes,
To dance lavoltas in the purple streams:
Sirens, with harps and silver psalteries,
Shall wait with music at thy frigate's stem,
And entertain fair Margaret with their lays.
England and England's wealth shall wait on thee;
Britain shall bend unto her prince's love,
And do due homage to thine excellence,
If thou wilt be but Edward's Margaret.

MARGARET

Pardon, my lord; if Jove's great royalty
Sent me such presents as to Danaë;
If Phœbus, 'tirèd in Latona's webs,
Came courting from the beauty of his lodge;
The dulcet tunes of frolic Mercury,
Nor all the wealth Heaven's treasury affords,
Should make me leave Lord Lacy or his love.

PRINCE EDWARD

I have learned at Oxford, then, this point of schools—
Abata causa, tollitur effectus:
Lacy, the cause that Margaret cannot love
Nor fix her liking on the English prince,
Take him away, and then th' effects will fail.—
Villain, prepare thyself; for I will bathe
My poniard in the bosom of an earl.

LACY

Rather than live, and miss fair Margaret's love,
Prince Edward, stop not at the fatal doom,
But stab it home: end both my loves and life.

MARGARET

Brave Prince of Wales, honoured for royal deeds,
'Twere sin to stain fair Venus' courts with blood;
Love's conquests ends, my lord, in courtesy:
Spare Lacy, gentle Edward; let me die,
For so both you and he do cease your loves.

PRINCE EDWARD
Lacy shall die as a traitor to his lord.

LACY
I have deserved it, Edward; act it well.

MARGARET
What hopes the prince to gain by Lacy's death?

PRINCE EDWARD
To end the loves 'twixt him and Margaret.

MARGARET
Why, thinks King Henry's son that Margaret's love
Hangs in th' uncertain balance of proud time?
That death shall make a discord of our thoughts!
No, slay the earl, and, 'fore the morning sun
Shall vaunt him thrice over the lofty east,
Margaret will meet her Lacy in the heavens.

LACY
If aught betides to lovely Margaret
That wrongs or wrings her honour from content,
Europe's rich wealth nor England's monarchy
Should not allure Lacy to over-live.
Then, Edward, short my life, and end her loves.

MARGARET
Rid me, and keep a friend worth many loves.

LACY
Nay, Edward, keep a love worth many friends.

MARGARET
And if thy mind be such as fame hath blazed,
Then, princely Edward, let us both abide
The fatal resolution of thy rage.
Banish thou fancy, and embrace revenge,
And in one tomb knit both our carcases,
Whose hearts were linkèd in one perfect love.

PRINCE EDWARD [Aside]
Edward, art thou that famous Prince of Wales,
Who at Damasco beat the Saracens,
And brought'st home triumph on thy lance's point?
And shall thy plumes be pulled by Venus down?
Is't princely to dissever lovers' leagues,

To part such friends as glory in their loves?
Leave, Ned, and make a virtue of this fault,
And further Peg and Lacy in their loves:
So in subduing fancy's passiön,
Conquering thyself, thou gett'st the richest spoil.—
Lacy, rise up. Fair Peggy, here 's my hand:
The Prince of Wales hath conquered all his thoughts,
And all his loves he yields unto the earl.
Lacy, enjoy the maid of Fressingfield;
Make her thy Lincoln Countess at the church,
And Ned, as he is true Plantagenet,
Will give her to thee frankly for thy wife.

LACY
Humbly I take her of my sovereign,
As if that Edward gave me England's right,
And riched me with the Albion diadem.

MARGARET
And doth the English prince mean true?
Will he vouchsafe to cease his former loves,
And yield the title of a country maid
Unto Lord Lacy?

PRINCE EDWARD
I will, fair Peggy, as I am true lord.

MARGARET
Then, lordly sir, whose conquest is as great,
In conquering love, as Caesar's victories,
Margaret, as mild and humble in her thoughts
As was Aspasia unto Cyrus self,
Yields thanks, and, next Lord Lacy, doth enshrine
Edward the second secret in her heart.

PRINCE EDWARD
Gramercy, Peggy:—Now that vows are past,
And that your loves are not to be revolt,
Once, Lacy, friends again. Come, we will post
To Oxford; for this day the king is there,
And brings for Edward Castile Elinor.—
Peggy, I must go see and view my wife:
I pray God I like her as I loved thee.
Beside, Lord Lincoln, we shall hear dispute
'Twixt Friar Bacan and learned Vandermast.—
Peggy, we'll leave you for a week or two.

MARGARET

As it please Lord Lacy; but love's foolish looks
Think footsteps miles and minutes to be hours.

LACY
I'll hasten, Peggy, to make short return.—
But please your honour go unto the lodge,
We shall have butter, cheese, and venison;
And yesterday I brought for Margaret
A lusty bottle of neat claret-wine:
Thus we can feast and entertain your grace.

PRINCE EDWARD
'Tis cheer, Lord Lacy, for an emperor,
If he respect the person and the place.
Come, let us in; for I will all this night
Ride post until I come to Bacon's cell.

[Exeunt.

SCENE IX

Oxford.

Enter **KING HENRY**, the **EMPEROR**, the **KING OF CASTILE**, **ELINOR**, **VANDERMAST**, and **FRIAR BUNGAY**.

EMPEROR
Trust me, Plantagenet, the Oxford schools
Are richly seated near the river-side:
The mountains full of fat and fallow deer,
The battling pastures lade with kine and flocks,
The town gorgeous with high-built colleges,
And scholars seemly in their grave attire,
Learnèd in searching principles of art.—
What is thy judgment, Jaques Vandermast?

VANDERMAST
That lordly are the buildings of the town,
Spacious the rooms, and full of pleasant walks;
But for the doctors, how that they be learnèd,
It may be meanly, for aught I can hear.

FRIAR BUNGAY
I tell thee, German, Hapsburg holds none such,
None read so deep as Oxenford contains;
There are within our academic state
Men that may lecture it in Germany

To all the doctors of your Belgic schools.

KING HENRY
Stand to him, Bungay, charm this Vandermast,
And I will use thee as a royal king.

VANDERMAST
Wherein dar'st thou dispute with me?

FRIAR BUNGAY
In what a doctor and a friar can.

VANDERMAST
Before rich Europe's worthies put thou forth
The doubtful question unto Vandermast.

FRIAR BUNGAY
Let it be this,—Whether the spirits of pyromancy or geomancy be most predominant in magic?

VANDERMAST
I say, of pyromancy.

FRIAR BUNGAY
And I, of geomancy.

VANDERMAST
The cabalists that write of magic spells,
As Hermes, Melchie, and Pythagoras,
Affirm that, 'mongst the quadruplicity
Of elemental essence, terra is but thought
To be a punctum squarèd to the rest;
And that the compass of ascending elements
Exceed in bigness as they do in height;
Judging the concave circle of the sun
To hold the rest in his circumference,
If, then, as Hermes says, the fire be greatest,
Purest, and only giveth shape to spirits,
Then must these demonès that haunt that place
Be every way superior to the rest.

FRIAR BUNGAY
I reason not of elemental shapes,
Nor tell I of the concave latitudes,
Noting their essence nor their quality,
But of the spirits that pyromancy calls,
And of the vigour of the geomantic fiends.
I tell thee, German, magic haunts the grounds,
And those strange necromantic spells,

That work such shows and wondering in the world,
Are acted by those geomantic spirits
That Hermes calleth terræ filii.
The fiery spirits are but transparent shades,
That lightly pass as heralds to bear news;
But earthly fiends, closed in the lowest deep,
Dissever mountains, if they be but charged,
Being more gross and massy in their power.

VANDERMAST
Rather these earthly geomantic spirits
Are dull and like the place where they remain;
For when proud Lucifer fell from the heavens,
The spirits and angels that did sin with him,
Retained their local essence as their faults,
All subject under Luna's continent.
They which offended less hung in the fire,
And second faults did rest within the air;
But Lucifer and his proud-hearted fiends
Were thrown into the centre of the earth,
Having less understanding than the rest,
As having greater sin and lesser grace.
Therefore such gross and earthly spirits do serve
For jugglers, witches, and vild sorcerers;
Whereas the pyromantic genii
Are mighty, swift, and of far-reaching power.
But grant that geomancy hath most force;
Bungay, to please these mighty potentates,
Prove by some instance what thy art can do.

FRIAR BUNGAY
I will.

EMPEROR
Now, English Harry, here begins the game;
We shall see sport between these learnèd men.

VANDERMAST
What wilt thou do?

FRIAR BUNGAY
Show thee the tree, leaved with refinèd gold,
Whereon the fearful dragon held his seat,
That watched the garden called Hesperidès,
Subdued and won by conquering Hercules.
Here Bungay conjures, and the tree appears with the dragon shooting fire.

VANDERMAST

Well done!

KING HENRY
What say you, royal lordings, to my friar?
Hath he not done a point of cunning skill?

VANDERMAST
Each scholar in the necromantic spells
Can do as much as Bungay hath performed!
But as Alcmena's bastard razed this tree,
So will I raise him up as when he lived,
And cause him pull the dragon from his seat,
And tear the branches piecemeal from the root.—
Hercules! Prodi, prodi, Hercules!

[HERCULES appears in his lion's skin.

HERCULES
Quis me vult?

VANDERMAST
Jove's bastard son, thou Libyan Hercules,
Pull off the sprigs from off th' Hesperian tree,
As once thou didst to win the golden fruit.

HERCULES
Fiat.

[Begins to break down the branches.

VANDERMAST
Now, Bungay, if thou canst by magic charm
The fiend, appearing like great Hercules,
From pulling down the branches of the tree,
Then art thou worthy to be counted learnèd.

FRIAR BUNGAY
I cannot.

VANDERMAST
Cease, Hercules, until I give thee charge.—
Mighty commander of this English isle,
Henry, come from the stout Plantagenets,
Bungay is learned enough to be a friar;
But to compare with Jaques Vandermast,
Oxford and Cambridge must go seek their cells
To find a man to match him in his art.
I have given non-plus to the Paduans,

To them of Sien, Florence, and Bologna,
Rheïms, Louvain, and fair Rotterdam,
Frankfort, Lutrech, and Orleans:
And now must Henry, if he do me right,
Crown me with laurel, as they all have done.

[Enter **FRIAR BACON**.

FRIAR BACON
All hail to this royal company,
That sit to hear and see this strange dispute!—
Bungay, how stands't thou as a man amazed.
What, hath the German acted more than thou?

VANDERMAST
What art thou that questions thus?

FRIAR BACON
Men call me Bacon.

VANDERMAST
Lordly thou look'st, as if that thou wert learned;
Thy countenance as if science held her seat
Between the circled arches of thy brows.

KING HENRY
Now, monarchs, hath the German found his match.

EMPEROR
Bestir thee, Jaques, take not now the foil,
Lest thou dost lose what foretime thou didst gain.

VANDERMAST
Bacon, wilt thou dispute?

FRIAR BACON
No,
Unless he were more learned than Vandermast:
For yet, tell me, what hast thou done?

VANDERMAST
Raised Hercules to ruinate that tree
That Bungay mounted by his magic spells.

FRIAR BACON
Set Hercules to work.

VANDERMAST

Now, Hercules, I charge thee to thy task;
Pull off the golden branches from the root.

HERCULES
I dare not. See'st thou not great Bacon here,
Whose frown doth act more than thy magic can?

VANDERMAST
By all the thrones, and dominatiöns,
Virtues, powers, and mighty hierarchies,
I charge thee to obey to Vandermast.

HERCULES
Bacon, that bridles headstrong Belcephon,
And rules Asmenoth, guider of the north,
Binds me from yielding unto Vandermast.

KING HENRY
How now, Vandermast, have you met with your match?

VANDERMAST
Never before was't known to Vandermast
That men held devils in such obedient awe.
Bacon doth more than art, or else I fail.

EMPEROR
Why, Vandermast, art thou overcome?—
Bacon, dispute with him, and try his skill.

FRIAR BACON
I come not, monarchs, for to hold dispute
With such a novice as is Vandermast;
I come to have your royalties to dine
With Friar Bacon here in Brazen-nose.
And, for this German troubles but the place,
And holds this audience with a long suspense,
I'll send him to his ácadémy hence.—
Thou Hercules, whom Vandermast did raise,
Transport the German unto Hapsburg straight,
That he may learn by travail, 'gainst the spring,
More secret dooms and aphorisms of art.—
Vanish the tree, and thou away with him!

[Exit **HERCULES** with **VANDERMAST** and the tree.

EMPEROR
Why, Bacon, whither dost thou send him?

FRIAR BACON

To Hapsburg: there your highness at return
Shall find the German in his study safe.

KING HENRY

Bacon, thou hast honoured England with thy skill,
And made fair Oxford famous by thine art.
I will be English Henry to thyself.
But tell me, shall we dine with thee to-day?

FRIAR BACON

With me, my lord; and while I fit my cheer,
See where Prince Edward comes to welcome you,
Gracious as is the morning-star of Heaven.

[Enter **PRINCE EDWARD, LACY, WARREN, ERMSBY**.

EMPEROR

Is this Prince Edward, Henry's royal son?
How martial is the figure of his face!
Yet lovely and beset with amorets.

KING HENRY

Ned, where hast thou been?

PRINCE EDWARD

At Framingham, my lord, to try your bucks
If they could scape the teasers or the toil.
But hearing of these lordly potentates,
Landed, and progressed up to Oxford town,
I posted to give entertain to them:
Chief to the Almain monarch; next to him,
And joint with him, Castile and Saxony
Are welcome as they may be to the English court.
Thus for the men: but see, Venus appears,
Or one that overmatcheth Venus in her shape!
Sweet Elinor, beauty's high-swelling pride,
Rich nature's glory and her wealth at once,
Fair of all fairs, welcome to Albion;
Welcome to me, and welcome to thine own,
If that thou deign'st the welcome from myself.

ELINOR

Martial Plantagenet, Henry's high-minded son,
The mark that Elinor did count her aim,
I liked thee 'fore I saw thee; now I love,
And so as in so short a time I may;
Yet so as time shall never break that so,

Found in the wealthy strand of Africa,
Shall royalize the table of my king.
Wines richer than th' Egyptian courtesan
Quaffed to Augustus' kingly countermatch,
Shall be caroused in English Henry's feast;
Candy shall yield the richest of her canes;
Persia, down her Volga by canoes,
Send down the secrets of her spicery;
The Afric dates, mirabolans of Spain,
Conserves and suckets from Tiberias,
Cates from Judaea, choicer than the lamp
That firèd Rome with sparks of gluttony,
Shall beautify the board for Frederick:
And therefore grudge not at a friar's feast.

[Exeunt.

SCENE X

Fressingfield.

Enter **LAMBERT** and **SERLSBY** with the **KEEPER**.

LAMBERT
Come, frolic Keeper of our liege's game,
Whose table spread hath ever venison
And jacks of wine to welcome passengers,
Know I'm in love with jolly Margaret,
That overshines our damsels as the moon
Darkeneth the brightest sparkles of the night.
In Laxfield here my land and living lies:
I'll make thy daughter jointer of it all,
So thou consent to give her to my wife;
And I can spend five-hundred marks a year.

SERLSBY
I am the lands-lord, Keeper, of thy holds,
By copy all thy living lies in me;
Laxfield did never see me raise my due:
I will enfeoff fair Margaret in all,
So she will take her to a lusty squire.

KEEPER
Now, courteous gentles, if the Keeper's girl
Hath pleased the liking fancy of you both,
And with her beauty hath subdued your thoughts,

'Tis doubtful to decide the question.
It joys me that such men of great esteem
Should lay their liking on this base estate,
And that her state should grow so fortunate
To be a wife to meaner men than you:
But sith such squires will stoop to keeper's fee,
I will, t' avoid displeasure of you both,
Call Margaret forth, and she shall make her choice.

LAMBERT
Content, Keeper; send her unto us.

[Exit **KEEPER**.

Why, Serlsby, is thy wife so lately dead,
Are all thy loves so lightly passèd over,
As thou canst wed before the year be out?

SERLSBY
I live not, Lambert, to content the dead,
Nor was I wedded but for life to her:
The grave ends and begins a married state.

[Enter **MARGARET**.

LAMBERT
Peggy, the lovely flower of all towns,
Suffolk's fair Helen, and rich England's star,
Whose beauty, tempered with her huswifery,
Makes England talk of merry Fressingfield!

SERLSBY
I cannot trick it up with poësies,
Nor paint my passions with comparisons;
Nor tell a tale of Phoebus and his loves.
But this believe me,—Laxfield here is mine,
Of ancient rent seven-hundred pounds a-year,
And if thou canst but love a country squire,
I will enfeoff thee, Margaret, in all.
I cannot flatter; try me, if thou please.

MARGARET
Brave neighbouring squires, the stay of Suffolk's clime,
A keeper's daughter is too base in gree
To match with men accompted of such worth.
But might I not displease, I would reply.

LAMBERT

And therefore so accept of Elinor.

KING OF CASTILE
Fear not, my lord, this couple will agree,
If love may creep into their wanton eyes.—
And therefore, Edward, I accept thee here,
Without suspence, as my adopted son.

KING HENRY
Let me that joy in these consorting greets,
And glory in these honours done to Ned,
Yield thanks for all these favours to my son,
And rest a true Plantagenet to all.

[Enter **MILES** with a cloth and trenchers and salt.

MILES
Salvete, omnes reges,
That govern your greges
In Saxony and Spain,
In England and in Almain!
For all this frolic rabble
Must I cover the table
With trenchers, salt, and cloth;
And then look for your broth.

EMPEROR
What pleasant fellow is this?

KING HENRY
'Tis, my lord, Doctor Bacon's poor scholar.

MILES [Aside]
My master hath made me sewer of these great lords; and, God knows, I am as serviceable at a table as a sow is under an apple-tree: tis no matter; their cheer shall not be great, and therefore what skills where the salt stand, before or behind?

[Exit.

KING OF CASTILE
These scholars know more skill in axioms,
How to use quips and sleights of sophistry,
Than for to cover courtly for a king.

[Re-enter **MILES** with a mess of pottage and broth; And, after him, **FRIAR BACON**.

MILES
Spill, sir? Why, do you think I never carried twopenny chop before in my life?—

By your leave, nobile decus,
For here comes Doctor Bacon's pecus,
Being in his full age
To carry a mess of pottage.

FRIAR BACON

Lordings, admire not if your cheer be this,
For we must keep our academic fare;
No riot where philosophy doth reign:
And therefore, Henry, place these potentates,
And bid them fall unto their frugal cates.

EMPEROR

Presumptuous friar! What, scoff 'st thou at a king?
What, dost thou taunt us with thy peasants' fare,
And give us cates fit for country swains?—
Henry, proceeds this jest of thy consent,
To twit us with a pittance of such price?
Tell me, and Frederick will not grieve thee long.

KING HENRY

By Henry's honour, and the royal faith
The English monarch beareth to his friend,
I knew not of the friar's feeble fare,
Nor am I pleased he entertains you thus.

FRIAR BACON

Content thee, Frederick, for I showed these cates
To let thee see how scholars use to feed;
How little meat refines our English wits.—
Miles, take away, and let it be thy dinner.

MILES

Marry, sir, I will.
This day shall be a festival-day with me;
For I shall exceed in the highest degree.

[Exit.

FRIAR BACON

I tell thee, monarch, all the German peers
Could not afford thy entertainment such,
So royal and so full of majesty,
As Bacon will present to Frederick.
The basest waiter that attends thy cups
Shall be in honours greater than thyself;—
And for thy cates, rich Alexandria drugs,
Fetched by carvels from Egypt's richest streights,

Say, Peggy; naught shall make us discontent.

MARGARET
Then, gentles, note that love hath little stay,
Nor can the flames that Venus sets on fire
Be kindled but by fancy's motiön.
Then pardon, gentles, if a maid's reply
Be doubtful, while I have debated with myself,
Who, or of whom, love shall constrain me like.

SERLSBY
Let it be me; and trust me, Margaret,
The meads environed with the silver streams,
Whose battling pastures fatneth all my flocks,
Yielding forth fleeces stapled with such wool
As Lemnster cannot yield more finer stuff,
And forty kine with fair and burnished heads,
With strouting dugs that paggle to the ground,
Shall serve thy dairy, if thou wed with me.

LAMBERT
Let pass the country wealth, as flocks and kine,
And lands that wave with Ceres' golden sheaves,
Filling my barns with plenty of the fields;
But, Peggy, if thou wed thyself to me,
Thou shalt have garments of embroidered silk,
Lawns, and rich net-works for thy head-attire:
Costly shall be thy fair habiliments,
If thou wilt be but Lambert's loving wife.

MARGARET
Content you, gentles, you have proffered fair,
And more than fits a country maid's degree:
But give me leave to counsel me a time,
For fancy blooms not at the first assault;
Give me but ten days' respite, and I will reply,
Which or to whom myself affectionates.

SERLSBY
Lambert, I tell thee, thou'rt importunate;
Such beauty fits not such a base esquire:
It is for Serlsby to have Margaret.

LAMBERT
Think'st thou with wealth to overreach me?
Serlsby, I scorn to brook thy country braves.
I dare thee, coward, to maintain this wrong,
At dint of rapier, single in the field.

SERLSBY
I'll answer, Lambert, what I have avouched.—
Margaret, farewell; another time shall serve.

[Exit.

LAMBERT
I'll follow.—Peggy, farewell to thyself;
Listen how well I'll answer for thy love.

[Exit.

MARGARET
How fortune tempers lucky haps with frowns,
And wrongs me with the sweets of my delight!
Love is my bliss, and love is now my bale.
Shall I be Helen in my froward fates,
As I am Helen in my matchless hue,
And set rich Suffolk with my face afire?
If lovely Lacy were but with his Peggy,
The cloudy darkness of his bitter frown
Would check the pride of these aspiring squires.
Before the term of ten days be expired,
Whenas they look for answer of their loves,
My lord will come to merry Fressingfield,
And end their fancies and their follies both:
Till when, Peggy, be blithe and of good cheer.

[Enter a **POST** with a letter and a bag of gold.

POST
Fair lovely damsel, which way leads this path?
How might I post me unto Fressingfield?
Which footpath leadeth to the Keeper's lodge?

MARGARET
Your way is ready, and this path is right.
Myself do dwell hereby in Fressingfield;
And if the Keeper be the man you seek,
I am his daughter: may I know the cause?

POST
Lovely, and once belovèd of my lord;
No marvel if his eye was lodged so low,
When brighter beauty is not in the heavens.—
The Lincoln Earl hath sent you letters here,
And, with them, just an hundred pounds in gold.

[Gives letter and bag.

Sweet, bonny wench, read them, and make reply.

MARGARET
The scrolls that Jove sent Danaë,
Wrapt in rich closures of fine burnished gold,
Were not more welcome than these lines to me,
Tell me, whilst that I do unrip the seals,
Lives Lacy well? How fares my lovely lord?

POST
Well, if that wealth may make men to live well.

MARGARET [Reads]
The blooms of the almond-tree grow in a night, and vanish in a morn; the flies hemera, fair Peggy, take
life with the sun, and die with the dew; fancy that slippeth in with a gaze, goeth out with a wink; and too
timely loves have ever the shortest length. I write this as thy grief, and my folly, who at Fressingfeld
loved that which time hath taught me to be but mean dainties: eyes are dissemblers, and fancy is but
queasy; therefore know, Margaret, I have chosen a Spanish lady to be my wife, chief waiting-woman to
the Princess Elinor; a lady fair, and no less fair than thyself, honourable and wealthy. In that I forsake
thee, I leave thee to thine own liking; and for thy dowry I have sent thee an hundred pounds; and ever
assure thee of my favour, which shall avail thee and thine much.
Farewell.
Not thine, nor his own,
Edward Lacy.

Fond Atè, doomer of bad-boding fates,
That wrapp'st proud fortune in thy snaky locks,
Didst thou enchant my birth-day with such stars
As lightened mischief from their infancy?
If heavens had vowed, if stars had made decree,
To show on me their froward influence,
If Lacy had but loved, heavens, hell, and all,
Could not have wronged the patience of my mind.

POST
It grieves me, damsel; but the earl is forced
To love the lady by the king's command.

MARGARET
The wealth combined within the English shelves,
Europe's commander, nor the English king,
Should not have moved the love of Peggy from her lord.

POST
What answer shall I return to my lord?

MARGARET
First, for thou cam'st from Lacy whom I loved,—
Ah, give me leave to sigh at very thought!—
Take thou, my friend, the hundred pounds he sent;
For Margaret's resolution craves no dower:
The world shall be to her as vanity;
Wealth, trash; love, hate; pleasure, despair:
For I will straight to stately Fremingham,
And in the abbey there be shorn a nun,
And yield my loves and liberty to God.
Fellow, I give thee this, not for the news,
For those be hateful unto Margaret,
But for thou'rt Lacy's man, once Margaret's love.

POST
What I have heard, what passions I have seen,
I'll make report of them unto the earl.

MARGARET
Say that she joys his fancies be at rest,
And prays that his misfortune may be hers.

[Exeunt.

SCENE XI

Friar Bacon's cell.

FRIAR BACON draws the curtains and is discovered in his cell, lying on a bed, with a white stick in one hand, a book in the other, and a lamp lighted beside him; and the Brazen Head, and **MILES** with weapons by him.

FRIAR BACON
Miles, where are you?

MILES
Here, sir.

FRIAR BACON
How chance you tarry so long?

MILES
Think you that the watching of the Brazen Head craves no furniture? I warrant you, sir, I have so armed myself that if all your devils come, I will not fear them an inch.

FRIAR BACON

Miles,
Thou know'st that I have divèd into hell,
And sought the darkest palaces of fiends;
That with my magic spells great Belcephon
Hath left his lodge and kneelèd at my cell;
The rafters of the earth rent from the poles,
And three-formed Luna hid her silver looks,
Trembling upon her concave continent,
When Bacon read upon his magic book.
With seven years' tossing necromantic charms,
Poring upon dark Hecat's principles,
I have framed out a monstrous head of brass,
That, by th' enchanting forces of the devil,
Shall tell out strange and uncouth aphorisms,
And girt fair England with a wall of brass.
Bungay and I have watched these threescore days,
And now our vital spirits crave some rest.
If Argus lived, and had his hundred eyes,
They could not over-watch Phobetor's night.
Now, Miles, in thee rests Friar Bacon's weal:
The honour and renown of all his life
Hangs in the watching of this Brazen Head;
Therefore I charge thee by th' immortal God,
That holds the souls of men within His fist,
This night thou watch; for ere the morning-star
Sends out his glorious glister on the north,
The head will speak: then, Miles, upon thy life,
Wake me; for then by magic art I'll work
To end my seven years' task with excellence.
If that a wink but shut thy watchful eye,
Then farewell Bacon's glory and his fame!
Draw close the curtains, Miles: now, for thy life,
Be watchful, and—

[Falls asleep.

MILES

So; I thought you would talk yourself asleep anon; and 'tis no marvel, for Bungay on the days, and he on the nights, have watched just these ten and fifty days: now this is the night, and 'tis my task, and no more. Now, Jesus bless me, what a goodly Head it is! and a nose! you talk of nos autem glorificare; but here's a nose that I warrant may be called nos autem populare for the people of the parish. Well, I am furnished with weapons; now, sir, I will set me down by a post, and make it as good as a watchman to wake me, if I chance to slumber. I thought, Goodman Head, I would call you out of your memento.

[**MILES** drifts off; his head hits the post, waking him.

Passion o' God, I have almost broke my pate!

[A great noise.

Up, Miles, to your task; take your brown-bill in your hand; here's some of your master's hobgoblins abroad.

THE HEAD
Time is.

MILES
Time is! Why, Master Brazen-head, have you such a capital nose, and answer you with syllables, "Time is"? Is this all my master's cunning, to spend seven years' study about "Time is"? Well, sir, it may be we shall have some better orations of it anon: well, I'll watch you as narrowly as ever you were watched, and I'll play with you as the nightingale with the slow-worm; I'll set a prick against my breast. Now rest there, Miles.

[**MILES** falls asleep, but is wakened by the prick.

Lord have mercy upon me, I have almost killed myself!

[A great noise.

Up, Miles; list how they rumble.

THE HEAD
Time was.

MILES
Well, Friar Bacon, you have spent your seven years' study well, that can make your head speak but two words at once, "Time was." Yea, marry, time was when my master was a wise man, but that was before he began to make the Brazen Head. You shall lie while your arse ache an your Head speak no better. Well, I will watch, and walk up and down, and be a peripatetian and a philosopher of Aristotle's stamp.

[A great noise.

What, a fresh noise? Take thy pistols in hand, Miles.

THE HEAD
Time is past.

[A lightning flashes forth, and a hand appears that breaks down the Head with a hammer.

MILES
Master, master, up! Hell's broken loose; your Head speaks; and there's such a thunder and lightning, that I warrant all Oxford is up in arms. Out of your bed, and take a brown-bill in your hand; the latter day is come.

[Bacon rises and comes forward.

FRIAR BACON
Miles, I come. O, passing warily watched!
Bacon will make thee next himself in love.
When spake the Head?

MILES
When spake the Head! did not you say that he should tell strange principles of philosophy?
Why, sir, it speaks but two words at a time.

FRIAR BACON
Why, villain, hath it spoken oft?

MILES
Oft! Ay, marry, hath it, thrice; but in all those three times it hath uttered but seven words.

FRIAR BACON
As how!

MILES
Marry, sir, the first time he said "Time is", as if Fabius Commentator should have pronounced a
sentence; [the second time] he said "Time was"; and the third time, with thunder and lightning, as in
great choler, he said, "Time is past."

FRIAR BACON
'Tis past indeed. Ah, villain! time is past:
My life, my fame, my glory, all are past.—
Bacon,
The turrets of thy hope are ruined down,
Thy seven years' study lieth in the dust:
Thy Brazen Head lies broken through a slave,
That watched, and would not when the Head did will.—
What said the Head first?

MILES
Even, sir, "Time is."

FRIAR BACON
Villain, if thou hadst called to Bacon then,
If thou hadst watched, and waked the sleepy friar,
The Brazen Head had uttered aphorisms,
And England had been circled round with brass.
But proud Astmeroth, ruler of the north,
And Demogorgon, master of the fates,
Grudge that a mortal man should work so much.
Hell trembled at my deep-commanding spells,
Fiends frowned to see a man their over-match;
Bacon might boast more than a man might boast!

But now the braves of Bacon have an end,
Europe's conceit of Bacon hath an end,
His seven years' practice sorteth to ill end:—
And, villain, sith my glory hath an end,
I will appoint thee to some fatal end.
Villain, avoid! Get thee from Bacon's sight!
Vagrant, go roam and range about the world,
And perish as a vagabond on earth!

MILES
Why, then, sir, you forbid me your service?

FRIAR BACON
My service, villain! with a fatal curse,
That direful plagues and mischief fall on thee.

MILES
'Tis no matter, I am against you with the old proverb,—the more the fox is cursed, the better he fares.
God be with you, sir: I'll take but a book in my hand, a wide-sleeved gown on my back, and a crowned
cap on my head, and see if I can want promotion.

FRIAR BACON
Some fiend or ghost haunt on thy weary steps,
Until they do transport thee quick to hell:
For Bacon shall have never merry day,
To lose the fame and honour of his Head.

[Exeunt.

SCENE XII

At Court.

Enter the **EMPEROR**, the **KING OF CASTILE**, **KING HENRY**, **ELINOR**, **PRINCE EDWARD**, **LACY**, and **RALPH
SIMNELL**.

EMPEROR
Now, lovely prince, the prime of Albion's wealth,
How fare the Lady Elinor and you?
What, have you courted and found Castile fit
To answer England in equivalence?
Will't be a match 'twixt bonny Nell and thee?

PRINCE EDWARD
Should Paris enter in the courts of Greece,
And not lie fettered in fair Helen's looks?

Or Phœbus scape those piercing amorets
That Daphne glancèd at his deity?
Can Edward, then, sit by a flame and freeze,
Whose heat puts Helen and fair Daphne down?
Now, monarchs, ask the lady if we gree.

KING HENRY
What, madam, hath my son found grace or no?

ELINOR
Seeing, my lord, his lovely counterfeit,
And hearing how his mind and shape agreed,
I came not, trooped with all this warlike train,
Doubting of love, but so affectionate,
As Edward hath in England what he won in Spain.

KING OF CASTILE
A match, my lord; these wantons needs must love!
Men must have wives, and women will be wed:
Let's haste the day to honour up the rites.

RALPH
Sirrah Harry, shall Ned marry Nell?

KING HENRY
Ay, Ralph: how then?

RALPH
Marry, Harry, follow my counsel: send for Friar Bacon to marry them, for he'll so conjure him and her
with his necromancy, that they shall love together like pig and lamb whilst they live.

KING OF CASTILE
But hearest thou, Ralph, art thou content to have Elinor to thy lady?

RALPH
Ay, so she will promise me two things.

KING OF CASTILE
What's that, Ralph?

RALPH
That she will never scold with Ned, nor fight with me.—Sirrah Harry, I have put her down with a thing
unpossible.

KING HENRY
What's that, Ralph?

RALPH

Why, Harry, didst thou ever see that a woman could both hold her tongue and her hands? no: but when egg-pies grow on apple-trees, then will thy grey mare prove a bag-piper.

EMPEROR
What says the Lord of Castile and the Earl of Lincoln, that they are in such earnest and secret talk?

KING OF CASTILE
I stand, my lord, amazèd at his talk,
How he discourseth of the constancy
Of one surnamed, for beauty's excellence,
The Fair Maid of merry Fressingfield.

KING HENRY
'Tis true, my lord, 'tis wondrous for to hear;
Her beauty passing Mars's paramour,
Her virgin's right as rich as Vesta's was.
Lacy and Ned hath told me miracles.

KING OF CASTILE
What says Lord Lacy? Shall she be his wife?

LACY
Or else Lord Lacy is unfit to live.—
May it please your highness give me leave to post
To Fressingfield; I'll fetch the bonny girl,
And prove, in true appearance at the court,
What I have vouchèd often with my tongue.

KING HENRY
Lacy, go to the 'querry of my stable,
And take such coursers as shall fit thy turn:
Hie thee to Fressingfield, and bring home the lass;
And, for her fame flies through the English coast,
If it may please the lady Elinor,
One day shall match your excellence and her.

ELINOR
We Castile ladies are not very coy;
Your highness may command a greater boon:
And glad were I to grace the Lincoln Earl
With being partner of his marriage-day.

PRINCE EDWARD
Gramercy, Nell, for I do love the lord,
As he that's second to thyself in love.

RALPH
You love her?—Madam Nell, never believe him you, though he swears he loves you.

ELINOR
Why, Ralph?

RALPH
Why, his love is like unto a tapper's glass that is broken with every touch; for he loved the fair maid of Fressingfield once out of all ho.—Nay, Ned, never wink upon me; I care not, I.

KING HENRY
Ralph tells all; you shall have a good secretary of him.—
But, Lacy, haste thee post to Fressingfield;
For ere thou hast fitted all things for her state,
The solemn marriage-day will be at hand.

LACY
I go, my lord.

[Exit.

EMPEROR
How shall we pass this day, my lord?

KING HENRY
To horse, my lord; the day is passing fair,
We'll fly the partridge, or go rouse the deer.
Follow, my lords; you shall not want for sport.

[Exeunt.

SCENE XIII

Friar Bacon's Cell.

Enter, to **FRIAR BACON** in his cell, **FRIAR BUNGAY**.

FRIAR BUNGAY
What means the friar that frolicked it of late,
To sit as melancholy in his cell
As if he had neither lost nor won to-day?

FRIAR BACON
Ah, Bungay, my Brazen Head is spoiled,
My glory gone, my seven years' study lost!
The fame of Bacon, bruited through the world,
Shall end and perish with this deep disgrace.

FRIAR BUNGAY

Bacon hath built foundation of his fame
So surely on the wings of true report,
With acting strange and uncouth miracles,
As this cannot infringe what he deserves.

FRIAR BACON

Bungay, sit down, for by prospective skill
I find this day shall fall out ominous:
Some deadly act shall 'tide me ere I sleep;
But what and wherein little can I guess.

FRIAR BUNGAY

My mind is heavy, whatsoe'er shall hap.

[Enter **TWO SCHOLARS**, sons to Lambert and Serlsby.

[Knock.

FRIAR BACON

Who's that knocks?

FRIAR BUNGAY

Two scholars that desire to speak with you.

FRIAR BACON

Bid them come in.
Now, my youths, what would you have?

1ST SCHOLAR

Sir, we are Suffolk-men and neighbouring friends;
Our fathers in their countries lusty squires;
Their lands adjoin: in Crackfield mine doth dwell,
And his in Laxfield. We are college-mates,
Sworn brothers, as our fathers live as friends.

FRIAR BACON

To what end is all this?

2ND SCHOLAR

Hearing your worship kept within your cell
A glass prospective, wherein men might see
Whatso their thoughts or hearts' desire could wish,
We come to know how that our fathers fare.

FRIAR BACON

My glass is free for every honest man.
Sit down, and you shall see ere long,

How or in what state your friendly fathers live.
Meanwhile, tell me your names.

1ST SCHOLAR
Mine Lambert.

2ND SCHOLAR
And mine, Serlsby.

FRIAR BACON
Bungay, I smell there will be a tragedy.

[Enter **LAMBERT** and **SERLSBY** with rapiers and daggers.

LAMBERT
Serlsby, thou hast kept thine hour like a man:
Thou'rt worthy of the title of a squire,
That durst, for proof of thy affectiön
And for thy mistress' favour, prize thy blood.
Thou know'st what words did pass at Fressingfield,
Such shameless braves as manhood cannot brook.
Ay, for I scorn to bear such piercing taunts,
Prepare thee, Serlsby; one of us will die.

SERLSBY
Thou see'st I single [meet] thee [in] the field,
And what I spake, I'll maintain with my sword.
Stand on thy guard, I cannot scold it out.
An if thou kill me, think I have a son,
That lives in Oxford in the Broadgates-hall,
Who will revenge his father's blood with blood.

LAMBERT
And, Serlsby, I have there a lusty boy,
That dares at weapon buckle with thy son,
And lives in Broadgates too, as well as thine.
But draw thy rapier, for we'll have a bout.

FRIAR BACON
Now, lusty younkers, look within the glass,
And tell me if you can discern your sires.

1ST SCHOLAR
Serlsby, 'tis hard; thy father offers wrong,
To combat with my father in the field.

2ND SCHOLAR
Lambert, thou liest, my father's is th' abuse,

And thou shall find it, if my father harm.

FRIAR BUNGAY
How goes it, sirs?

1ST SCHOLAR
Our fathers are in combat hard by Fressingfield.

FRIAR BACON
Sit still, my friends, and see the event.

LAMBERT
Why stand'st thou, Serlsby? doubt'st thou of thy life?
A veney, man! fair Margaret craves so much.

SERLSBY
Then this for her.

1ST SCHOLAR
Ah, well thrust!

2ND SCHOLAR
But mark the ward.

[They fight and kill each other.

LAMBERT
O, I am slain!

[Dies.

SERLSBY
And I,—Lord have mercy on me!

[Dies.

1ST SCHOLAR
My father slain!—Serlsby, ward that.

2ND SCHOLAR
And so is mine!—Lambert, I'll quite thee well.

[The **TWO SCHOLARS** stab each other, and die.

FRIAR BUNGAY
O strange stratagem!

FRIAR BACON

See, friar, where the fathers both lie dead!—
Bacon, thy magic doth effect this massacre:
This glass prospective worketh many woes;
And therefore seeing these brave lusty brutes,
These friendly youths, did perish by thine art,
End all thy magic and thine art at once.
The poniard that did end the[ir] fatal lives,
Shall break the cause efficiat of their woes.
So fade the glass, and end with it the shows
That necromancy did infuse the crystal with.

[He breaks the glass.

FRIAR BUNGAY
What means learned Bacon thus to break his glass?

FRIAR BACON
I tell thee, Bungay, it repents me sore
That ever Bacon meddled in this art.
The hours I have spent in pyromantic spells,
The fearful tossing in the latent night
Of papers full of necromantic charms,
Conjuring and abjuring devils and fiends,
With stole and alb and strange pentaganon;
The wresting of the holy name of God,
As Sother, Eloïm, and Adonai,
Alpha, Manoth, and Tetragrammaton,
With praying to the five-fold powers of Heaven,
Are instances that Bacon must be damned
For using devils to countervail his God.—
Yet, Bacon, cheer thee, drown not in despair:
Sins have their salves, repentance can do much:
Think Mercy sits where Justice holds her seat,
And from those wounds those bloody Jews did pierce,
Which by thy magic oft did bleed afresh,
From thence for thee the dew of mercy drops,
To wash the wrath of high Jehovah's ire,
And make thee as a new-born babe from sin.—
Bungay, I'll spend the remnant of my life
In pure devotion, praying to my God
That He would save what Bacon vainly lost.

[Exeunt.

SCENE XIV

Fressingfield.

Enter **MARGARET** in Nun's apparel, the **KEEPER**, and their **FRIEND**.

KEEPER
Margaret, be not so headstrong in these vows:
O, bury not such beauty in a cell,
That England hath held famous for the hue!
Thy father's hair, like to the silver blooms
That beautify the shrubs of Africa,
Shall fall before the dated time of death,
Thus to forgo his lovely Margaret.

MARGARET
Ah, father, when the harmony of Heaven
Soundeth the measures of a lively faith,
The vain illusions of this flattering world
Seem odious to the thoughts of Margaret.
I lovèd once,—Lord Lacy was my love;
And now I hate myself for that I loved,
And doted more on him than on my God,—
For this I scourge myself with sharp repents.
But now the touch of such aspiring sins
Tells me all love is lust but love of heavens;
That beauty used for love is vanity.
The world contains naught but alluring baits,
Pride, flattery, and inconstant thoughts.
To shun the pricks of death, I leave the world,
And vow to meditate on heavenly bliss,
To live in Framingham a holy nun,
Holy and pure in conscience and in deed;
And for to wish all maids to learn of me
To seek Heaven's joy before earth's vanity.

FRIEND
And will you, then, Margaret, be shorn a nun, and so leave us all?

MARGARET
Now farewell world, the engine of all woe!
Farewell to friends and father! Welcome Christ!
Adieu to dainty robes! This base attire
Better befits an humble mind to God
Than all the show of rich habiliments.
Farewell, O love! and, with fond love, farewell
Sweet Lacy, whom I lovèd once so dear!
Ever be well, but never in my thoughts,
Lest I offend to think on Lacy's love:
But even to that, as to the rest, farewell!

[Enter **LACY**, **WARREN** and **ERMSBY**, booted and spurred.

LACY
Come on, my wags, we're near the Keeper's lodge.
Here have I oft walked in the watery meads,
And chatted with my lovely Margaret.

WARREN
Sirrah Ned, is not this the Keeper?

LACY
'Tis the same.

ERMSBY
The old lecher hath gotten holy mutton to him: a nun, my lord.

LACY
Keeper, how far'st thou? holla, man, what cheer?
How doth Peggy, thy daughter and my love?

KEEPER
Ah, good my lord! O, woe is me for Peggy!
See where she stands clad in her nun's attire,
Ready for to be shorn in Framingham.
She leaves the world because she left your love.
O, good my lord, persuade her if you can!

LACY
Why, how now, Margaret! What, a malcontent?
A nun! What holy father taught you this,
To task yourself to such a tedious life
As die a maid! 'Twere injury to me,
To smother up such beauty in a cell.

MARGARET
Lord Lacy, thinking of my former miss,
How fond the prime of wanton years were spent
In love (O, fie upon that fond conceit,
Whose hap and essence hangeth in the eye!)
I leave both love and love's content at once,
Betaking me to Him that is true love,
And leaving all the world for love of Him.

LACY
Whence, Peggy, comes this metamorphosis?
What, shorn a nun, and I have from the court
Posted with coursers to convey thee hence

To Windsor, where our marriage shall be kept!
Thy wedding-robes are in the tailor's hands.
Come, Peggy, leave these péremptory vows.

MARGARET
Did not my lord resign his interest,
And make divorce 'twixt Margaret and him?

LACY
'Twas but to try sweet Peggy's constancy.
But will fair Margaret leave her love and lord?

MARGARET
Is not Heaven's joy before earth's fading bliss,
And life above sweeter than life in love?

LACY
Why, then, Margaret, will be shorn a nun?

MARGARET
Margaret
Hath made a vow which may not be revoked.

WARREN
We cannot stay, my lord; an if she be so strict,
Our leisure grants us not to woo afresh.

ERMSBY
Choose you, fair damsel, yet the choice is yours:—
Either a solemn nunnery or the court,
God or Lord Lacy: which contents you best,
To be a nun or else Lord Lacy's wife?

LACY
A good motion.—Peggy, your answer must be short.

MARGARET
The flesh is frail: My lord doth know it well,
That when he comes with his enchanting face,
Whate'er betide, I cannot say him nay.
Off goes the habit of a maiden's heart,
And, seeing fortune will, fair Fremingham,
And all the show of holy nuns, farewell!
Lacy for me, if he will be my lord.

LACY
Peggy, thy lord, thy love, thy husband.
Trust me, by truth of knighthood, that the king

Stays for to marry matchless Elinor,
Until I bring thee richly to the court,
That one day may both marry her and thee.—
How say'st thou, Keeper? Art thou glad of this?

KEEPER
As if the English king had given
The park and deer of Fressingfield to me.

ERMSBY
I pray thee, my Lord of Sussex, why art thou in a brown study?

WARREN
To see the nature of women; that be they never so near God, yet they love to die in a man's arms.

LACY
What have you fit for breakfast? We have hied
And posted all this night to Fressingfield.

MARGARET
Butter and cheese, and umbles of a deer,
Such as poor keepers have within their lodge.

LACY
And not a bottle of wine?

MARGARET
We'll find one for my lord.

LACY
Come, Sussex, let us in: we shall have more,
For she speaks least, to hold her promise sure.

[Exeunt.

SCENE XV

Somewhere in Europe.

Enter a **DEVIL** seeking **MILES**.

DEVIL
How restless are the ghosts of hellish sprites,
When every charmer with his magic spells
Calls us from nine-fold-trenchèd Phlegethon,
To scud and over-scour the earth in post

Upon the speedy wings of swiftest winds!
Now Bacon hath raised me from the darkest deep,
To search about the world for Miles his man,
For Miles, and to torment his lazy bones
For careless watching of his Brazen Head.
See where he comes: O, he is mine.

[Enter **MILES** in a gown and a corner-cap.

MILES
A scholar, quoth you! marry, sir, I would I had been made a bottle-maker when I was made a scholar; for I can get neither to be a deacon, reader, nor schoolmaster, no, not the clerk of a parish. Some call me a dunce; another saith my head is as full of Latin as an egg's full of oatmeal: thus I am tormented, that the devil and Friar Bacon haunt me.—Good Lord, here's one of my master's devils! I'll go speak to him.—What, Master Plutus, how cheer you?

DEVIL
Dost thou know me?

MILES
Know you, sir! why, are not you one of my master's devils, that were wont to come to my master, Doctor Bacon, at Brazen-nose?

DEVIL
Yes, marry, am I.

MILES
Good Lord, Master Plutus, I have seen you a thousand times at my master's, and yet I had never the manners to make you drink. But, sir, I am glad to see how conformable you are to the statute.—I warrant you, he's as yeomanly a man as you shall see: mark you, masters, here's a plain honest man, without welt or guard.—But I pray you, sir, do you come lately from hell?

DEVIL
Ay, marry: how then?

MILES
Faith, 'tis a place I have desired long to see: have you not good tippling-houses there? May not a man have a lusty fire there, a pot of good ale, a pair of cards, a swingeing piece of chalk, and a brown toast that will clap a white waistcoat on a cup of good drink?

DEVIL
All this you may have there.

MILES
You are for me, friend, and I am for you.
But I pray you, may I not have an office there!

DEVIL

Yes, a thousand: what wouldst thou be?

MILES
By my troth, sir, in a place where I may profit myself. I know hell is a hot place, and men are marvellous dry, and much drink is spent there; I would be a tapster.

DEVIL
Thou shall.

MILES
There's nothing lets me from going with you, but that 'tis a long journey, and I have never a horse.

DEVIL
Thou shalt ride on my back.

MILES
Now surely here's a courteous devil, that, for to pleasure his friend, will not stick to make a jade of himself.—But I pray you, goodman friend, let me move a question to you.

DEVIL
What's that?

MILES
I pray you, whether is your pace a trot or an amble?

DEVIL
An amble.

MILES
'Tis well; but take heed it be not a trot: but 'tis no matter, I'll prevent it.

[Puts on spurs.

DEVIL
What dost?

MILES
Marry, friend, I put on my spurs; for if I find your pace either a trot or else uneasy, I'll put you to a false gallop; I'll make you feel the benefit of my spurs.

DEVIL
Get up upon my back.

[**MILES** mounts on the **DEVIL'S** back.

MILES
O Lord, here's even a goodly marvel, when a man rides to hell on the devil's back!

[Exeunt, the **DEVIL** roaring.

At Court.

Enter in a Procession:

I. First the **EMPEROR** with a pointless sword;

II. Next the **KING OF CASTILE** carrying a sword with a point;

III. **LACY** carrying the globe;

IV. **PRINCE EDWARD**;

V. **WARREN** carrying a rod of gold with a dove on it;

VI. **ERMSBY** with a crown and scepter;

VII. **PRINCESS ELINOR**, with...

VIII. **MARGARET**, Countess of Lincoln on her left hand;

IX. **KING HENRY**;

X. **FRIAR BACON**;

XI. and **LORDS** attending.

PRINCE EDWARD
Great potentates, earth's miracles for state,
Think that Prince Edward humbles at your feet,
And, for these favours, on his martial sword
He vows perpetual homage to yourselves,
Yielding these honours unto Elinor.

KING HENRY
Gramercies, lordings; old Plantagenet,
That rules and sways the Albion diadem,
With tears discovers these conceivèd joys,
And vows requital, if his men-at-arms,
The wealth of England, or due honours done
To Elinor, may quite his favourites.—
But all this while what say you to the dames
That shine like to the crystal lamps of Heaven?

EMPEROR

If but a third were added to these two,
They did surpass those gorgeous images
That gloried Ida with rich beauty's wealth.

MARGARET

'Tis I, my lords, who humbly on my knee
Must yield her orisons to mighty Jove
For lifting up his handmaid to this state;
Brought from her homely cottage to the court,
And graced with kings, princes, and emperors,
To whom (next to the noble Lincoln Earl)
I vow obedience, and such humble love
As may a handmaid to such mighty men.

ELINOR

Thou martial man that wears the Almain crown,
And you the western potentates of might,
The Albion princess, English Edward's wife,
Proud that the lovely star of Fressingfield,
Fair Margaret, Countess to the Lincoln Earl,
Attends on Elinor,—gramercies, lord, for her,—
'Tis I give thanks for Margaret to you all,
And rest for her due bounden to yourselves.

KING HENRY

Seeing the marriage is solémnizèd,
Let's march in triumph to the royal feast,—
But why stands Friar Bacon here so mute?

FRIAR BACON

Repentant for the follies of my youth,
That magic's secret mysteries misled,
And joyful that this royal marriäge
Portends such bliss unto this matchless realm.

KING HENRY

Why, Bacon,
What strange event shall happen to this land?
Or what shall grow from Edward and his queen?

FRIAR BACON

I find by deep presciënce of mine art,
Which once I tempered in my secret cell,
That here where Brute did build his Troynovant,
From forth the royal garden of a king
Shall flourish out so rich and fair a bud,

Whose brightness shall deface proud Phœbus' flower,
And over-shadow Albion with her leaves.
Till then Mars shall be master of the field,
But then the stormy threats of wars shall cease:
The horse shall stamp as careless of the pike,
Drums shall be turned to timbrels of delight;
With wealthy favours plenty shall enrich
The strand that gladded wandering Brute to see,
And peace from Heaven shall harbour in these leaves
That gorgeous beautify this matchless flower:
Apollo's heliotropion then shall stoop,
And Venus' hyacinth shall vail her top;
Juno shall shut her gilliflowers up,
And Pallas' bay shall bash her brightest green;
Ceres' carnation, in consort with those,
Shall stoop and wonder at Diana's rose.

KING HENRY
This prophecy is mystical.—
But, glorious commanders of Europa's love,
That make fair England like that wealthy isle
Circled with Gihon and swift Euphrates,
In royalizing Henry's Albion
With presence of your princely mightiness:—
Let 's march: the tables all are spread,
And viands, such as England's wealth affords,
Are ready set to furnish out the boards.
You shall have welcome, mighty potentates:
It rests to furnish up this royal feast,
Only your hearts be frolic; for the time
Craves that we taste of naught but jouissance.
Thus glories England over all the west.

[Exeunt **OMNES**.

Omne tulit punctum qui miscuit utile dulci.

Robert Greene - A Short Biography

Robert Greene was, by the best accounts available, born in Norwich in 1558 and baptised on July 11th.

As can be understood much of his early life was not recorded and few contemporary accounts exist to add to what we know. Greene is believed to have attended Norwich Grammar School but did attend Cambridge and received his in 1580, and an M.A. in 1583. He took no part, that we know of, in any of the Cambridge university dramatic productions. Academically he seemed to be nothing above fair. For his B.A. he graduated 38th out of the 41 students in his college, and 115th out of the total graduating class of 1580 of 205 students. For his M.A. it is believed, but not entirely proven, that he transferred to Clare College and was placed 5th out of the 12 students there, and 29th of the 129 students at the university graduating in that year.

But life was about to change. He moved to London and began an extraordinary chapter in his life and career as a widely published author. He was prolific, and of quality, publishing across many genres such as romances, plays and autobiography.

Greene's literary career began with the publication of the long romance, Mamillia, which was entered in the Stationers' Register on 3rd October 1580. Greene's romances were written in a highly wrought style which reached its peak in Pandosto (1588) and Menaphon (1589). Short poems and songs that he incorporated in some of the romances attest to his ability as a lyric poet. One song from Menaphon, 'Weep not my wanton, smile upon my knee, (a mother's lullaby to her baby son)', enjoyed immense success.

Within the space of a few years Greene had published over twenty-five works in prose across several genres and is regarded as 'England's first celebrity author'.

In 1588, he was granted an MA from Oxford University, almost certainly as a courtesy degree. Thereafter he sometimes placed the phrase 'Utruisq. Academiae in Artibus Magister', 'Master of Arts in both Universities' on the title page of his works.

As previously mentioned enough facts on Greene's life are not available so much is made of his autobiographical work 'The Repentance of Robert Greene', In it, Greene claimed to have travelled to Italy and Spain; however, no evidence of Greene's continental trip has been found. Indeed, some scholars doubt that 'The Repentance of Robert Greene' was actually written by the man himself.

In another section of the book Greene claimed to have married a gentleman's daughter, whom he abandoned after having had a child by her and spent her dowry, after which she went to Lincolnshire, and he to London. In 'Four Letters and Certain Sonnets' (1592), Gabriel Harvey prints a letter allegedly written by Greene to his wife in which he addresses her as 'Doll'. However, research through the ages has failed to find any further evidence or record of this marriage. Perhaps it really is indeed a complete fiction and not even by him.

According to 'The Repentance of Robert Greene', Greene is alleged to have written 'A Groatsworth of Wit Bought with a Million of Repentance' during the month leading up to his death, including in it a letter to his wife asking her to forgive him and writing that he was sending their son back to her.

No record of facts survives to validate this. Again in 'Four Letters and Certain Sonnets', Gabriel Harvey claimed that Greene kept a mistress, Em, the sister of a criminal known as 'Cutting Ball' and later hanged at Tyburn. She is described as 'a sorry ragged quean of whom Greene had his base son Infortunatus Greene'.

The facts may be hidden but thankfully much of his work survives. He was perhaps one of the first English authors to support himself with his pen in an age when professional authorship was virtually unknown.

In his 'coney-catching' pamphlets, Greene portrays himself as a well-known public figure, narrating colourful inside stories of rakes and rascals duping young gentlemen and solid citizens out of their hard-earned money. These stories, told from the perspective of a repentant former rascal, have been considered autobiographical, and have been thought to incorporate many facts of Greene's own life thinly veiled as fiction: his early riotous living, his marriage and desertion of his wife and child for the sister of a notorious character of the London underworld, his dealings with players, and his success in the production of plays for them. However, the alternate account suggests that Greene invented almost everything, part of his undoubted skills of being a writer.

In addition to his prose works, Greene also wrote several plays, none of them published in his lifetime, including 'The Scottish History of James IV', 'Alphonsus', and his greatest popular success, 'Friar Bacon and Friar Bungay', as well as 'Orlando Furioso', based on Ludovico Ariosto's Orlando Furioso.

His plays earned himself the title as one of the 'University Wits', including George Peele, Thomas Nashe, and Christopher Marlowe.

As was common with the better talents of the time many works were latter attributed to their hand by unscrupulous printers and publishers eager to put a better name on the title page in their pursuit of sales. Greene has been proposed as the author of several dramas, including a second part to 'Friar Bacon' which may survive as 'John of Bordeaux', 'The Troublesome Reign of King John', 'George a Greene', 'Fair Em', 'A Knack to Know a Knave', 'Locrine', 'Selimus', and 'Edward III', and even Shakespeare's 'Titus Andronicus' and 'Henry VI' plays.

Greene is most familiar to Shakespeare scholars for his pamphlet Greene's 'Groats-Worth of Wit', which alludes to a line, "O tiger's heart wrapped in a woman's hide", found in Shakespeare's Henry VI, Part 3 (c. 1591–92):

'... for there is an upstart Crow, beautified with our feathers, that with his Tygers hart wrapt in a Players hyde, supposes he is as well able to bombast out a blanke verse as the best of you: and being an absolute Johannes fac totum, is in his owne conceit the onely Shake-scene in a countrey.'

Greene's complaint of an actor who states he can write as well as university-educated playwrights, alludes to the actor with a quote that appears in both the True Tragedy quarto and Shakespeare's Folio version of Henry VI, Part 3, and uses the term 'Shake-scene', a unique term never used before or after Greene's screed, to refer to the actor.

Robert Greene died 3rd September 1592, at the very young age of 34.

His death and burial were announced by Gabriel Harvey in a letter to Christopher Bird of Saffron Walden dated 5th September, first published as a 'butterfly pamphlet' about 8th September, and later expanded as 'Four Letters and Certain Sonnets', entered in the Stationers' Register on 4th December 1592.

However, no record of Greene's burial has ever been found.

Prose works

Mamillia: A Mirror or Looking-glass for the Ladies of England (1583)
Mamillia: The Second Part of the Triumph of Pallas (1593)
The Anatomy of Lovers' Flatteries (1584)
The Myrrour of Modestie (1584)
Arbasto; The Anatomy of Fortune (1584)
Gwydonius; The Card of Fancy (1584)
The Debate Between Folly and Love (1584)
The Second Part of the Tritameron of Love (1587)
Planetomachia (1585)
An Oration or Funeral Sermon (1585)
Morando; The Tritameron of Love (1587)
Morando; The Second Part of the Tritameron of Love (1587)
Euphues: His Censure to Philautus (1587)
Greene's Farewell to Folly (1591)
Penelope's Web (c1587)
Alcida; Greene's Metamorphosis (1617)
Greenes Orpharion (1599)
Pandosto (1588)
Perimedes (1588)
Ciceronis Amor (1589)
Menaphon (1589)
The Spanish Masquerado (1589)
Greene's Mourning Garment (1590)
Greene's Never Too Late (1590)
Francesco's Fortunes, or The Second Part of Greene's Never Too Late (1590)
Greene's Vision, Written at the Instant of his Death (c1590)
The Royal Exchange (1590)
A Notable Discovery of Coosnage (1591)
The Second Part of Conycatching (1591)
The Black Books Messenger (1592)
A Disputation Between a Hee Conny-Catcher and a Shee Conny-Catcher (1592)
A Groatsworth of Wit Bought with a Million of Repentance (1592)
Philomela (1592)
A Quip for an Upstart Courtier (1592)
The Third and Last Part of Conycatching (1592)

Verse

A Maiden's Dream (1591)

Plays

Friar Bacon and Friar Bungay (circa 1590)
The History of Orlando Furioso (circa 1590)
A Looking Glass for London and England (with Thomas Lodge) (circa 1590)
The Scottish History of James the Fourth (circa 1590)
The Comical History of Alphonsus, King of Aragon (circa 1590)

Selimus (circa 1594)